Advance Praise for *The Debt-Free Spending Plan*

"A riveting debt-breakthrough and a great read. In the world of debt-free living, this book is a trailblazer!"

—Stephen Dover, International Chief Investment
Officer, Franklin Templeton Global Advisers

"*The Debt-Free Spending Plan* offers real-world, practical, and pragmatic advice to help those struggling to balance their cash inflows and outflows. In minutes each day and without a lot of technical mumbo-jumbo, JoAnneh teaches us to set goals, stop racking up debt, and create long-lasting financial security. I loved reading this book and will recommend it to many in need of its wisdom!"

—Mary Crawford, Professor, Stanford Continuing
Studies Program, Values-Based Life & Wealth
Planning and Twenty-First Century Retirement

"If you're struggling with debt or can't get your money under control, following JoAnneh's plan will get you on the right track ASAP! *The Debt-Free Spending Plan* provides a great, easy-to-understand system for getting a grip on anyone's finances."

—Trent Hamm, author of *The Simple Dollar: How One Man
Wiped Out His Debts and Achieved the Life of His Dreams*

THE DEBT-FREE SPENDING PLAN

The Debt-Free Spending Plan

An Amazingly Simple Way to Take
Control of Your Finances Once and for All

JOANNEH NAGLER

AMACOM AMERICAN MANAGEMENT ASSOCIATION
New York • Atlanta • Brussels • Chicago • Mexico City
San Francisco • Shanghai • Tokyo • Toronto • Washington, D.C.

This publication is designed to provide accurate and authoritative information in regard to the subject matter covered. It is sold with the understanding that the publisher is not engaged in rendering legal, accounting, or other professional service. If legal advice or other expert assistance is required, the services of a competent professional person should be sought.

Library of Congress Cataloging-in-Publication Data

Nagler, JoAnneh.
  The debt-free spending plan : an amazingly simple way to take control of your finances once and for all / JoAnneh Nagler.
    p. cm.
Includes bibliographical references and index.
ISBN-13: 978-0-8144-3243-3
ISBN-10: 0-8144-3243-3
1. Finance, Personal. 2. Consumer debt. 3. Budgets, Personal. I. Title.
HG179.N33 2012
332.024'02—dc23

2012010889

About AMA
American Management Association (www.amanet.org) is a world leader in talent development, advancing the skills of individuals to drive business success. Our mission is to support the goals of individuals and organizations through a complete range of products and services, including classroom and virtual seminars, webcasts, webinars, podcasts, conferences, corporate and government solutions, business books, and research. AMA's approach to improving performance combines experiential learning—learning through doing—with opportunities for ongoing professional growth at every step of one's career journey.

Printing number
10 9 8 7 6 5 4 3 2

This book is dedicated to Theresa Hanneman Boer, who encouraged me to write it, to Bonita Banducci, who helped me learn to live debt-free, and to Michael Nagler, with whom all good things in my life are possible.

CONTENTS

This is a book for people who are in debt and don't know how to live within their means. It's a book for people who spend and don't know where their money's going. It's a book for people who hate numbers, never liked math, and rarely—if ever—balance their checkbook.

The Debt-Free Spending Plan is a simple program that will help all of us who have had money trouble stop incurring debt, live on what we earn, and begin building our dreams. "Dream building" is the most important part of this book. Most of us who are pressed by debt or have a lack of clarity about our spending feel we have no opportunity to build anything—let alone our dreams. We go from year to year in a tightly wound survival mode, and we don't feel as if there's ever any financial breathing room to plan for things that are truly meaningful to us.

The Debt-Free Spending Plan will help you change all of that. You will learn to live—and live well—on what you earn, on what you're bringing in. You'll learn to use your creativity rather than your credit cards. You'll have a plan to cover your living expenses that addresses all of your needs, including entertainment money, vacation money, and "fun money" to spend however you like. You'll have a debt-repayment plan that won't control your spending or your life. And you won't have to live on canned soup and crackers.

You'll finally—and for good—rid yourself of money stress.

■　■　■

"That sounds terrific," you say, "but there are stacks of finance books out there that promise the same thing. So what's so different about this one?" This is what's different about this book: It's simple. It doesn't require that you sift through chapters of high-minded financial advice. It doesn't call for an anthropological dig into your past spending history or your childhood. It doesn't ask for knowledge of any specific software, nor does it belabor you with a history of the credit industry. It assumes you need help right now with your debt and spending issues and it gives that to you.

This book offers easy, *daily* strategies for working with your expenses and needs. It teaches you simple tracking mechanisms that keep you solvent. It gives you foolproof tools to help you when you do the inevitable and overspend. And it does *all* of that in the first thirty days of using it.

Most of us who have debt problems pick up finance and investment books, and put them down before we finish the first chapter. These books assume we know too much. They tell us the "downside" of debt but don't tell us how to get out of it—or worse yet, don't help us create tools that will help us stop racking up debt. This book does. It's clear, straightforward, and uncomplicated. It's designed for the eight-year-old in us who froze up in math class and never recovered.

In the process of defining our money dilemmas, I have used a few words in this book that are not necessarily grammatically correct or in mainstream usage. You'll see me refer to a "debtor," and use *debting* as an active verb (that's you when you're in debt, or when you're actively running up debt). You'll also see me refer to "self-deprivation" as a term to describe those of us who incur debt for some of our needs and then hold out on other needs—a concept that you may not be familiar with regarding your finances. This is the best way I know to get my point across without using cumbersome language, so let the message serve you.

In any helping profession, there has to be an ethic of "Take what works and dump the rest." I make certain admonitions and particular statements that have been true for me and my clients, but ultimately, you will have to decide what works for you and what doesn't. I've crafted the Debt-Free Spending Plan as a unique tool—not for a general public, but specifically for those of us who have trouble with debt, trouble with spending, and trouble feeling that we have a grasp on our money.

Use what works for you; leave the rest at the table. In the end, it's not about your adopting something I've created, in some A+ way. It's about your using the tools that work for you to get free of money stress and begin enjoying your life again.

I have crafted my approach to debt-free living from my personal experience and from those I have worked with. Yet I stand on the shoulders of many who have gone before me and from whom I have gained valuable insights—authors, individual friends, acquaintances, and support group participants, as well as seminars on money and prosperity. (Some are referenced in the text; some I have learned from in principle.) Certainly, any spending plan or budget will have similar sections and categories. *The Debt-Free Spending Plan*, however, is original in its approach, like a recipe that uses common ingredients combined uniquely for a new flavor. It is designed to be simple, approachable, and easy to understand.

∎　∎　∎

If *The Debt-Free Spending Plan* works well for you, I'd love to hear your stories. Feel free to use the e-mail link on my Web site at www.debtfreespendingplan.com. Thank you for giving me the opportunity to offer you what I have learned about living debt-free. It's changed my life in amazing ways, and I trust it will change yours, too.

INTRODUCTION

I WAS 42 YEARS old, standing in the grocery-store line with an overfilled basket of food that I was going to pay for with a credit card that had over $28,000 on it. After shopping, I'd go get a cash advance of another $3,000 to pay my rent and bills. My small writing business was tanking. I had seven other cards that I was juggling, for a grand total of about $80,000—and it would be another few months before I racked up $10,000 more in fees and cash advances. I had hives. I had nightmares. Just looking at the groceries in my basket made me nauseous. I had run up more than $55,000 of my debt publishing a music CD and waiting for a miracle to happen. I had run up the rest in living expenses, ignoring my business. I had no idea what I was spending—I just put it all on the cards.

I'd been in debt before—most of my life, actually—but it had never gotten this bad. I couldn't believe I'd let my debt get so out of hand. I couldn't believe I'd become so irresponsible with my money. Standing in the grocery-store line, I started to hyperventilate. *What the hell had I been thinking?* I couldn't breathe. I had to stop debting—I had to find a way to stop my hideous cycle of running up credit card debt—but I didn't know how. And I didn't have a clue where to begin.

Sound familiar?

Debt is a killer. It's a drag on our hearts and minds, an energy hog, and a full-time guilt-making machine. It leads us in only one direction: Down, into lives of worry, fear, and desperation. Even a little bit of debt can cause us enough grief to agonize over, our heads swirling in sleeplessness when we should be resting, our stomachs tied in knots whenever we think about our finances.

We know—as anyone who has ever been in debt knows—the downside of being in over our heads financially. It's uncomfortable. It's painful. We can feel it right now, in our gut, and we don't even have to conjure up the details of it. Most likely it's caused us to stay up nights, grind our teeth, sweat bullets, overeat, have indigestion, break out in hives, or some other version of physical or spiritual discomfort.

We know what it's doing to us. But the worst part about debting is that it's not just exacting psychological and physical payments for what we've done in the past. The horrendous worry comes from the fact that *we are still doing it*. We are in debt, we keep debting, and we don't see a way out. *Our expenses are greater than our income*, we say. So what else can we do?

We can even argue that we feel okay about it—"it's just a board game," "what's the big deal?" "I front myself money, then I pay it back later. . . ." But we all know that being in debt does not produce feelings of peace and well-being. If we've dug ourselves a hole, debting against our home-equity line, running up credit cards or project debting (as I did), these rationalizations just make our guilt and self-loathing worse.

We can get philosophical and argue that the debting machine of *credit* produces income for our economy—that it's "just the way things get done" in our cultural timeline, and we're just a cog in the wheel. We *have* to use credit cards. We *have* to be part of the machine. And even while we vent such justifications, we take no pleasure in being in debt, and we surely do not feel industrious for having accrued it. And most of the time, we have no idea how we're going to pay all that money back.

So instead of feeling engaged and a part of our lives, we find ourselves yearning for the proverbial "one day" when we might (1) make twice as much money as we're making now, (2) get bailed out by an inheritance, (3) get a big pay-off from a "minor" car accident, (4) find a bag of cash by the side of the road, or, depending on the magnitude of the amount we owe, (5) escape to Bogotá for a lifelong visit. "One day" makes us feel trapped today, and a lot of the joy we could be experiencing in daily life vaporizes into worry over debt.

We may have tried credit consolidators, borrowing from parents or friends, or getting an extra job to pay off creditors, and even when we have been able to zero those balances out, a year, two years, four years later we're in debt again. "How did this happen?" we lament.

This is how it happened.

We got ourselves into debt for one simple reason: *We have no spending plan.* We have no idea how much it *really* costs us to live, what we're able to live on, and what "wants" and "needs" we can afford. We think budgets are constricting and want no part of them, but our lack of spending clarity causes us even greater grief. We're afraid that if we look deeply into our finances we'll never have another luxury or fulfilled want for the rest of our lives.

The Debt-Free Spending Plan will help you end all of that. It will help you take simple steps to stop running up debt, live within your means, and start building something that's meaningful to you. It will offer you guideposts to funding what you *want*, as well as what you need. It's easy to use and specifically designed for people who tune out when it comes to their money.

It does not require that you learn a special computer program. It does not require that you live on noodles and toast. It does not require any special skills besides the use of a calculator and basic addition and subtraction. And it doesn't matter whether you make $14,000 or $14 million. If you can add, you can use the Debt-Free Spending Plan to live free from debt for the rest of your life. I'm not kidding. If you've had enough of the pain that comes from living in debt, then read on. If you want to live free of worry over money and start *choosing* where you spend your cash, then read on.

. . .

This book is for everyone, everywhere, who has believed that money wisdom belongs to a special class of people with a special class of skills. It doesn't. It's yours for the taking right here in *The Debt-Free Spending Plan*.

1

. . . . .

The Heart of Our Debting Issues

IN THE PAST two decades, a plethora of books on personal finance have hit our best-seller lists. Almost all of them tell us to get out of debt, to live on a budget, and to invest. They deliberate the reasons why debt is a "bad investment"—that is, we pay much more for products and services because of interest and inflation—but these books almost never tell us how, *specifically*, to get out of debt *and* how to stop going into debt. They tell us that having a budget is a necessity, but they don't tell us how to create and *live by one*—a realistic daily one. Some straight-talking authors give readers monthly bottom lines and even delineate spending categories, but nobody—I mean nobody!—

gives a practical, *daily* strategy to help us stop our compulsiveness and live within our means.

Most finance books tell us to make investments. And that's all very nice and neat for those of us who believe we are responsible financially or who are motivated by money math. But for those of us who are already in debt or are in spending trouble, this kind of advice is disastrous.

Invest? Who are you kidding? We can barely make our rent and credit card bills each month. We owe the IRS two years of back taxes. *Retirement?* We shrink at the very word. *Pay ourselves first?* In what dream world? *Budget?* Come on! We can't bring ourselves to write down on paper what we already think we know—that we don't have enough to live on and we're carelessly overspending anyway.

So those of us who need financial coaching the most tune out, turn off, and close these books for good, almost as soon as we open them. And if we're in the cycle of debt—entitlement, addictive overspending, guilt, and regret—these financial admonitions most often make us feel more of what we already feel: that our finances are always a disaster, so it's best to put our heads in the sand and grind through this money experience as blindly as possible.

The Debt-Free Spending Plan Is Not a Budget

The Debt-Free Spending Plan is not a traditional budget. It's not a shortage-inducing tool. It's a simple plan to show you, first, how you are currently spending your money, and then—more importantly— asks you how you *want* to spend what you have.

This book asks you to write some things down. It asks you to use your calculator. It asks you to be realistic about paying your bills— like rent, mortgage, and health insurance—first. And then it helps you create a daily living expense plan that includes all of your needs, and even some of your wants. It helps you nail down the octopus arms of your unaddressed debts (Chapter 6), and begin paying them back, even if it's just $5 a month. It helps you address your living expenses first, so you can learn to live on your income without deprivation, without living for your creditors.

In doing these few simple tasks, you'll begin to get clarity. And with clarity comes more money. I've coached many people, helping them create their personal Debt-Free Spending Plans, and each has had some small or large "money miracle" as a result. It's almost as if life were saying, "Okay, Jo, you're taking good care of the money you've got now, so we're going to give you some more. We trust you to use it well." Do the Debt-Free Spending Plan and see for yourself. More responsibility with your money breeds a greater capacity to handle more of it.

LIVING WELL ON WHAT YOU EARN

Here's the crux of the argument: When you learn that you really can afford what you need and want, and you can support yourself without going into debt, you will feel better about yourself. You will stop the roller-coaster of self-abuse and self-hatred, and start building a new relationship with yourself and your money—a debt-free relationship that builds pride and self-respect.

The Debt-Free Spending Plan may require that you visit the bank a few more times in the first few months. It will require that you set aside time at the end of each month to add and subtract some numbers. And for the price of a little time and some jotted-down numbers, you'll begin to get free.

The promise of the Debt-Free Spending Plan is very simple: You'll get free of money stress, and you'll live more richly and more fully. You'll make choices about how you want to live and how you want to spend. You'll have a plan to address each of your debts. You'll relax. And, probably the biggest payoff I've seen in myself and my coaching clients is, *you will no longer fight about money in your relationships.*

You'll have a Spending Plan to address your Bills (monthly payments), your Daily Needs (groceries, cleaners, medical co-pays), your wants (entertainment, vacations, fun money)—and will actually have some reserves. Yes, you'll start saving, even if it's just $10 a month, for things you like, things you enjoy, things you want. And you'll do all of that in the first thirty days of using the Debt-Free Spending Plan.

Even if this sounds impossible to you—if your finances are in such a disastrous state that you can't imagine being at peace with your money—the Debt-Free Spending Plan will still work for you. The Spending Plan doesn't care if you're afraid, rebellious, skeptical, or angry. If you do the plan, it will work. Every time.

What This Book Will Do for You

The Debt-Free Spending Plan is not a book to teach you how to invest. It's not a book that will tell you the ins and outs of credit lines or credit ratings. It's not a book that's meant to educate you about the overall American financial situation or world financial picture. It's not a book to help convince you of the spirituality of money, or how to attract it—though by living debt-free you will automatically do just that.

Similarly, the Debt-Free Spending Plan is not a pie-in-the-sky, "put your spiritual needs first" approach to money. It's not a plan that asks you to "visualize your way into prosperity." It addresses, first, what feels most realistic to you. Rent. Food. Living expenses. When I was $90,000 in debt, facing bankruptcy, and my business was falling apart, the last thing I wanted to hear was an admonition to put my "spiritual" and "educational" needs first. I needed to figure out how to live! I needed to figure out how to pay for my housing, my health care, my utilities, and to deal with the creditors at my back.

I'm not a believer in advocating that risky-for-debtors proposition "Do what you love and the money will follow." While the premise is sound enough for people who have good money skills—do something that's meaningful to you, get paid for it, live within your means, and build on that—for debtors this advice can be disastrous. That's because we debtors will twist this encouraging adage to mean we should *spend money we don't have* to do what we love—and then God, or the Universe, or the Great Magical Money Machine in the sky will relieve us of our financial burden (our debt) because we went into debt for something we love. We use this admonition to *gamble*, running up our credit lines. I've done it and I know dozens more people who've done it, too, with disastrous results.

So the Debt-Free Spending Plan will not ask you to engage in magical thinking and unfounded financial risks in the name of "spiritual prosperity." *It is not a spiritual principle to incur debt in order to do what you love.* The Debt-Free Spending Plan will teach you to take steady steps in building your dreams, and to fully fund your personal, familial, entrepreneurial, and artistic ventures as you undertake them.

That's a hard pill to swallow for those of us who are used to using debt to fund our ventures. We want a payoff *now*, and we want it to occur simply because we took the risk of trying something we believe in. But using credit this way is risking our solvency, and it's just another justification for incurring debt—this time with a spiritual spin. Don't fall for it. There's another way, and it's infinitely more peaceful.

Most personal finance books give some detailed version of one or all of the above topics—useful, in my opinion, in the hands of someone who's not debting. But for those of us who are running up debt (or who are living in cycles of it), the first order of business is to *learn how to live solvent.* That means living with the money we have, each and every month. It means learning how to live in the black, month after month, until this way of earning and spending becomes an ingrained part of our very being.

How Did I Get into This Mess?

Answering the question "How did I get into debt trouble?" is murky terrain for most of us. First, we're often in more trouble with money than we like to admit. We may already know that we have a tendency to overspend or be vague about our finances, and we probably don't have a realistic grasp on what it costs us to live or the total amounts we owe. That's all normal stuff when we begin learning to live debt-free.

But the heart of our issues—the real trouble, if we're honest about it—is that we keep running up debt even after we know we're in over our heads. We're still using credit cards to live even after we've glimpsed the impending financial disasters ahead. We don't like to take responsibility for the messy (or even disastrous) state of our finances, and we have a trunk full of reasons that debting has been necessary. We feel *compelled* to debt even though we know it is causing us harm. And even when we pay off all of our cards and begin debting again with the best of intentions—that is, a promise to pay off all of our cards each month—we end up back in terrible, escalating debt. So how did we get into these nasty debt habits in the first place? We're going to take a look at that right now.

THE RISE OF THE CREDIT CULTURE

I used to joke in the 1980s—when my debt troubles began—that if I had it, I spent it, and if I didn't, I spent it anyway. When I was 20 years old, ATM cards were just appearing and only a few businesses took credit cards (you couldn't buy groceries with credit cards), but there were certainly enough credit options for people to begin getting into debt. And I did.

Now we can buy anything on credit! We can even run up cash advances and pay our mortgages with a card! In other words, those of us from age 20 to 50 are the first generations in our history who have had ready access to credit since we reached adulthood. With that development came the resulting freedom to extend our income beyond its reasonable reach, and that has radically impacted the way we buy.

This is not our parents' doing. This is not something our teachers neglected to teach us. We did this. This is our part. Our generations invented this system, thought it was incredibly peachy, and we promoted it until the cows came home. Who is "everywhere you are"? Your credit card company. What is "priceless"? Whatever your credit card can buy.

So what have we done with the illustrious spending freedom that's been bestowed upon us? This is what we've done: We've created a country full of people *of all* ages with financial disasters on their hands, with more money pressure than is reasonable for any one human being to handle.

IN WITH STRUCTURE, OUT WITH STRINGENCY

Our misuse of credit freedom reminds me of the disaster in class scheduling that my high school implemented in 1974. I was a freshman, and our progressive superintendent decided to institute what was called "modular scheduling"—an open class-scheduling program in which students had huge blocks of free time to schedule as they wished.

We were to use—*at our own leisure*—"learning labs," "resource centers," and the library. All we had to do was make a list at the beginning of the day of where we were supposed to be at each hour. And—this was the kicker—we had entire mornings, whole afternoons, and sometimes whole days completely free of assigned classes to attend. You can guess what happened. A huge number of teenagers started spending entire days smoking pot in the woods behind the school. Having no structure was okay for a handful of kids who had amazing self-discipline and well-developed skills, but for a lot of my high school peers, it was a debacle that tanked rather quickly.

The same has been true, in my opinion, for our generation regarding credit. Structure-less and free to run up as much debt as we can qualify for, we've done just that. We're the high-schoolers smoking behind the school. Without any limits, we've failed to hold ourselves accountable. Having no structure has not been good for us. In fact, it's been a disaster. We're clueless about how much we spend, how much we need, what we can afford, and how to spend wisely. We're not accountable to ourselves or our creditors, and we have no idea how to live in peace with our money.

We need structure. Not stringency, but *structure*. We need a structure that's strong, yet flexible enough for real-life money concerns, for the actual items that come up in a week or a month of spending. And we need enough flexibility in our structure for the real-life financial glitches that come from just being human.

AM I A DEBTOR?

Probably one of the hardest things to admit to ourselves is that we're debtors. What's a "debtor"? A debtor is someone who uses unsecured debt to fund living expenses, purchases, needs, wants, and even "emergencies." What's "unsecured debt"? Credit cards, lines of credit, department store cards, borrowing from friends or family—in short, any purchase, borrowing, or loan that indebts us to another person or institution, with interest or without, in which we owe money that we do not currently have.

A "secured debt," by contrast, is a house or a car—an item that, if given back to the financial institution that offered the loan, would erase the debt. (That's a *theoretical* definition. These days, even a house or a car may not be considered a secured debt. Houses purchased on interest-only loans before the market dropped are no longer "secured" because the house is worth less than the amount owed.) Debtors who refinance and *live on* their equity are essentially debting against their "secured" loan. Giving back a car may or may not erase the debt, depending on the bank's or dealer's default policies. Financed refrigerators, furniture, TVs, computer equipment, and household appliances all qualify as unsecured debt.

So—are we debtors? Do we use credit cards? Do we use department store cards? Do we borrow from parents, siblings, or friends?

Then we're debtors. Do we use credit lines or credit agencies? We're debtors. Do we spend any money that we currently do not have? We're debting! It doesn't matter what it's for. Is it for a new business? For art? A spiritual quest? "Emergencies"? We're still debtors. Debt doesn't care about the reasons; all debt cares about is one thing: *Do you owe?* Owing is the cause of our financial stress. We owe more than we have, more than we earn, more than we can possibly, reasonably pay back on our current income and still meet our daily needs.

So say it out loud: "I'm a debtor." Then write it down. Try it in front of the mirror. Have the courage to look yourself in the eye and say, "I'm a debtor. I'm in debt." If you don't know how you're going to pay your debt back, say that, too. "I don't know how I'm going to pay back the money I owe."

Saying it out loud may sound daunting, but admitting this is the first step in moving toward a solution. If you have no debt now, but you've had to crawl out of debt at least twice in your life, say it: "I'm a debt cycler. I go in and out of debt." If you're not in debt but you don't know where your money goes or you regularly overspend, then say that out loud. It doesn't matter what the level of your financial distress is. *The Debt-Free Spending Plan can help.*

Great. Good job. You've been honest with yourself. That's enough. Now, what are we going to do about it?

WE REALLY CAN FUND OUR NEEDS

We all have a right to enough good food, enough decent clothing, enough to pay our bills, enough for entertainment and a vacation (because that's what makes for a healthy, stress-free life), and of course, enough for a small pleasure or two. Those are the financial components that make for an engaged, productive living experience. Most of us with debt trouble have never learned these skills, so we have to learn them now. Time to get started!

YOUR PSYCHOLOGICAL SPENDING ISSUES
WILL NOT STAND IN YOUR WAY

The first thing I realized in creating the Debt-Free Spending Plan was that I had some issues about the way I spent my living-expenses money. A decade ago, I was spending over $800 a month on groceries—not including dining out. Now, I like to cook, but I have a lean body frame and a healthy eating style, and I could clearly see that it was probably not possible for me to eat $800 worth of groceries by myself each month, in addition to dining out. I was having a great time shopping, and a lovely time cooking, and I was *giving away a lot of food*, as well as letting plenty of good food go bad.

More important, I only had about $950 each month to live on after I paid my bills, so $800 for food was way too much money to be spending on one expense item. I was shopping out of *habit*, and it made me feel taken care of. I shopped like my mother had shopped—only she had been buying food for a family of six. What I would have rather had, instead of all those groceries, was a travel fund, a paid-for dental visit, a timely car tune-up, or a new dress—things I went into debt for, out of rebellion, because I believed I didn't have enough money for them. My lack of clarity had me blowing a bunch of cash each month on expenses that weren't of any particular use to me. That's money that I could have been using for things that were much more meaningful.

The same thing was true with my household items—stuff like tile cleaners, light bulbs, floor wax. Once, when I was on a rampage about my lack of spending clarity, I collected all of the household items under all my sinks and in all my closets, and I averaged the cost of everything I was buying in a year. I calculated that I was spending over $125 a month on everything from shoe polish to Ajax. And I had no savings. I had no medical expense fund. I had no monthly clothing allotment. The $125 was a significant monthly amount for me on my after-bills money. Yet I bought the most expensive household cleaners and couldn't pay for a vacation.

You get the picture. There's a *psychology* to how and why we spend. And as you're looking at your spending patterns, you'll see what you're doing psychologically. But don't get stuck there. Your lack of clarity is all you're interested in noting here. You don't need to belabor your psychology or go on an archeological dig into your childhood.

The Debt-Free Spending Plan is a neutral tool. *It doesn't care how you got the spending habits you have or who you acquired them from.* If your parents were miserly, it won't stop you from doing the Debt-Free Spending Plan. If your grandmother held money over your head and now you spend more than you earn in rebellion, it's not going to stop you from getting clarity with the Plan. There is no psychological quest required to ferret out the root of your spending habits. That's the beauty of the Debt-Free Spending Plan. It's about getting clarity *now*.

THE FLIP SIDE OF OVERSPENDING: SELF-DEPRIVATION

When I was introduced to the concept of self-deprivation, my immediate response was, "I'm not a self-depriver—I overspend all the time. I'm in debt for God's sake!" But looking a little more closely at my spending patterns, I realized I had serious self-deprivation issues.

I had no allotments for medical bills, emergencies, and no savings. I hadn't seen the dentist regularly in several years. I had a couple of good years when I paid cash for vacations, and then guiltily put subsequent getaways on my credit cards. My car needed a tune-up. The heater had been broken in my apartment for four years. It took me looking straight into the face of a bankruptcy budget form to realize that clothing is a *necessity*.

I had been treating clothes like luxury items because I love them—believing I had to "steal" from my food, rent, and credit card payments money in order to buy clothes. Truthfully, I had almost always put my clothing expenses on credit cards. It never occurred to me to have a monthly necessity amount set aside. And I never thought to have "fun money" that I could use however I chose.

I suddenly realized what self-deprivation looks like and the role debt plays in it. Without clarity on the amounts we can spend on our needs, we debt to fund them, often overspending. Our cycles of debting put pressure on us, and so we deprive ourselves in areas like medical and dental care, clothing, savings, vacations, and entertainment—all things we can't quite seem to account for in our monthly spending, but that we know help to make up a healthy and contented life.

And here's the kicker: A lot of the time we're charging things that should be a regular part of our monthly spending. In other words, if we weren't in a cycle of deprivation, debt, and overspending, we'd actually have some cash to fund what we need! More important, we may believe that our "wants" have to be relegated to the "if I win the lottery" category. So instead of having a plan for our wants—depriving ourselves again—we go without, and eventually rebel, and run up more credit card debt. "Extra" cash, we believe, has to be used for debt payments or a financial emergency—like our car breaking down. We never consider that funding our wants is part of a healthy lifestyle. *That's* self-deprivation.

So, What Have I Been Spending, Anyway?

The obvious next question is, *How hard is it going to be to figure out what I've been spending?* I promise you will not have to compose an analytical treatise on your expenditures to work the Debt-Free Spending Plan. That's why the Spending Plan is divided into simple categories and focuses on current spending.

But here's the underlying premise that will save you from yourself: *Don't try to have clarity for the past. Just have clarity for today.* Do not try to account for your spending for the past four years. Do not try to go over every receipt from the last tax year. Do not try to balance your checkbook from even last month! Please keep this admonition close at hand while you begin: *Just have clarity for today.* That's all. We've lived with financial chaos for years and years, it's true, but going backwards is not going to help us.

Having clarity just for today may seem a little wobbly at first, because you may feel the compulsion to go backwards in time to clear up this or that. Don't do it. Spending hours trying to find the lost $154.36 in your checking account from two months ago is not going to help. Start fresh, from today. Give yourself that dignity. Over the course of a few months, you'll start to have a new base with clear numbers, a new history. That's enough. Killing yourself to solve the mystery of your financial past will only get in the way of your willingness to work the Debt-Free Spending Plan.

KEEP IT SIMPLE

The Debt-Free Spending Plan is going to help you get clarity with your numbers. But it won't take a constitution-writing effort to create one. I don't believe in complicated spending plans that require sixty subcategories of daily expenses. I don't know about you, but I have money issues. If a plan is too complicated for me, I'm just going to get bored and give up. One of the reasons I got into financial trouble in the first place was because I believed that charts and graphs and financial planning were tools for other people with different skills than me. So I can't go there.

Some plans have us detailing four to five subcategories of expenses under "Food," "Personal Care," and so on, so that each category prompts several more categories to keep track of. Use them if they work for you. But if they don't, you need to know that the Debt-Free Spending Plan is crafted with you in mind. It's designed to be very easy to use and simple to track your spending. You've already got issues with your finances, and probably bigger issues with keeping numbers. The more complicated it all gets, the more likely you will be to check out. So the objective here is to keep things simple.

DON'T WAIT UNTIL YOU LEARN A FINANCIAL SOFTWARE PACKAGE

If you already use Quicken or QuickBooks (or something like it), you can easily set up the Debt-Free Spending Plan in your program. Or, you can use a financial app or a spreadsheet. You can also use a Word document, make a list, and add up your numbers at the end of the month. (It takes about five minutes.) Or, you can write them down by hand on graph paper. It doesn't matter.

But don't wait until you learn a financial software package to start the Debt-Free Spending Plan. If you think you have to know Quicken before you get started, you'll never begin. Trust me. I can't tell you how many times I've sat in a financial seminar with a group of debtors who were desperately trying to get a grip on their finances by learning a new software program. (Desperation can make you deaf to all new learning. It can shut down any capacity for mathematics you ever had and make you forget how to add.) Learn the program or don't learn the program. But start the Debt-Free Spending Plan anyway, and *first*.

But, if you love technology and can't wait to put your personal Debt-Free Spending Plan into an app or program, just remember that a *tracking tool* alone is not going to get you solvent. No matter how you track what you spend, you must have a planning mechanism for each month in order to get out of debt. So, before you go out shopping for some cool new app, learn and adopt the principles of living debt-free.

IF YOU HATE TECHNOLOGICAL TOOLS

Here's my suggestion to those of you who shut down around technology and money issues: Make it work for the 8-year-old in you. Make it work for a kid of 8 or 10 who's gotten freaked out by not being great in math class and has blocked out numbers ever since. Make a list (on paper or in a Word document), add up the numbers, and call it a day. If you're more sophisticated than that and have a computer-savvy sensibility, and you have experience with financial software packages, then use what you know. But if you don't—if you hate learning computer stuff—then just list your numbers. Otherwise, you will never begin. And beginning is what will open the gates to clarity, and clarity brings you freedom.

THE TROUBLE WITH TRACKING

Maybe you already know how you spend and what you spend. Most of us who are in debt don't, but let's say you do. You already write your numbers down someplace or have them in a bookkeeping program on your laptop. Great. You'll probably feel one step ahead. But tracking isn't enough. Tracking your monthly expenditures doesn't do anything toward *planning*. I can track all day long, and it's still not going to stop me from overspending at the grocery store. I can list everything I spend on household goods and still never put aside anything for buying a house, for replacing my old computer or for my CD recording fund. I can *know* what I spend and still deprive myself of medical and dental needs, vacations, clothing, savings, and so on.

Here's the trouble with a tracking-only approach to the numbers: We're spending, but we have no map of how to spend or what's financially meaningful to us. It's like sailing rudderless through our financial seas. We spend, but our needs go unaddressed. We track, but it doesn't get us much more clarity in the end than if we hadn't. We have an idea of what we're doing with our money, but we're not accountable to anything more than writing down a lump-sum total of what we've spent.

I've known lots of people who have tracked their numbers for years and still never achieve solvency. They still spend beyond their means and deprive themselves in specific areas in which they have genuine needs. And, most important, they have remained *blocked for years* in the dream-building category, unable to fund what was truly most important to them. Tracking will not give you ultimate clarity. Planning will. That's the whole point of the Debt-Free Spending Plan.

Stop Debting, One Day at a Time

This is the huge crux of it, isn't it? *How, on God's green earth, do we stop the cycle of our debting?* In other words, how can we possibly stop racking up credit card debt when we (1) owe almost as much as we earn, (2) can't make our monthly payments, or (3) have no job?

First, realize that it's never convenient to stop debting. Generally, the people I know who've decided to stop debting have no reasonable financial sign from the heavens that this is the time. They just decide, and they stop. And then they get support to craft their lives around the money they have and the money they make. That's what the Debt-Free Spending Plan is for. To teach you how to live—and then live well—on what you make, on what you bring in.

Usually, those of us who've decided to stop debting have hit some kind of brick wall, or have "hit bottom" with our own behavior. We've had enough. We're sick of ourselves and our snowballing financial disasters. We're willing to try something else besides our own dead-end scheming. We've had no peace for so long—possibly our whole adult lives—that we're finally, mercifully, ready to find some way to live within our means.

No one says this is going to be easy. But to make it work you are going to have to stop using credit cards, stop borrowing for your living expenses. That's going to sound like an ultimatum, and those of us with money issues don't like to be told what to do. But our rebellion is what got us into our spend-into-debt situation in the first place. So if this is the place where you get off the train, consider this: What has your best thinking gotten you so far? Overwhelming debt? A stressed-out life? Pressure and guilt every time you buy something—even something as simple as your groceries? Has your best thinking gotten you a restful night's sleep after you use credit cards and then try to pay your bills? Has it made your relationships peaceful regarding money?

My guess is you can answer just about all of these questions with a big, fat *No!* So I'm going to ask you for your willingness to try another way of thinking. We've all heard the expression that insanity is doing the same thing over and over and expecting a different result. So I'm going to ask you to gather up *all* of your credit cards, and put them in the freezer. Really. Freeze them, quite literally. Just for now. I mean *all* of them. Don't save even one. (You'll say it's for "emergencies," but you're a debtor and you'll surely use it for something less than a life-and-death situation.) Get them out of your reach or cut them up and get rid of them altogether.

If you're not willing right now, then be willing to be willing. That means you'll open-heartedly take a look at what not debting would look like for you—possibly by doing what I call "The Science Experiment." That is, you'll do it for a while—say, two or three months—just to see what will happen, in an empirical sort of way. Just to get some data and get back to yourself later on the results.

Can you work the Debt-Free Spending Plan and continue to debt? *Not well.* You can get some clarity, sure, and you can get a grip on what you're spending. But if you continue to debt you will hang your efforts at solvency fairly quickly. Tell the truth: The reason you're reading this book is that you know you have to give up credit cards and borrowing—you just don't know how. The Debt-Free Spending Plan is going to show you how. For now all you have to do is be willing to agree that you'll stop using credit and borrowing to live.

DON'T LET EXCUSES STAND IN YOUR WAY

We're—each of us—going to think we can't stop using credit. We've got "reasons." We've got special circumstances. Maybe we really believe that nobody has it as bad as we do. We *have to* debt. But in the end, our "reasons" for debting just don't matter. There's nothing special about us that entitles us to ruin our health, our well-being, our family life, or our relationships by running up debt.

Almost all of us have been in debt at some time in our lives. It's not unique. There are recessions, job losses, and medical disasters that send us debting. There are underpaying jobs, child-rearing demands, retirement changes, entrepreneurial and artistic ventures, and "transition times" that send us into debt. There are addictive issues—overshopping, hoarding, cluttering—that compel us to debt. There are stances ("I hated math so I won't do my numbers"), excuses ("My father manipulated me by withholding money and I'm never going to be that way"), and just plain rebellion. Take a look around. Running up debt is not so special. There are tens of thousands of us who've done it and more who are still doing it. We don't need any more excuses. What we need is help—specific support for living within our means, for putting down our credit cards and never picking them up again. What we need is a road map for learning how to live decently—even *well*—on what we earn. The Debt-Free Spending Plan is that road map.

YOUR HISTORY DOES NOT ABSOLVE YOU OF THE NEED FOR CLARITY

Though we could spend all day going over the reasons we debt and live beyond our means (they're as multitudinous as the number of debtors on the planet), for most of us the common denominator is our history—that is, what we were taught and what we *weren't* taught.

There's a saying that goes, "Hurt people hurt people," meaning that if we've been hurt or injured, we'll tend to impose the same behavior on someone else, or turn it inward, hurting ourselves. Once we realize that we were not properly guided regarding our finances—that we were "hurt" by never being schooled in money skills and that it's affected our ability to move well in the world—we still have the responsibility to learn these skills *now*, whether we were taught them or not. Otherwise, we will hurt those we love with our money issues, just as our parents or teachers hurt us. The important thing to note is that we don't get to wallow in whatever we missed as kids. If our parents didn't have the skills to train us to live debt-free, then we have to train ourselves. Their world was different from our world.

What's possible for us financially was not possible for them financially. *So, the buck stops here.* Literally.

The Debt-Free Spending Plan is a present-moment tool. So, if we're hiding behind "I wasn't given the skills to do well with money," here's a news flash: Almost no one got great money counseling. That doesn't absolve us of the need for money clarity in our lives right now. And, should we choose to avoid learning that clarity, we will most surely hurt the ones we love, without doubt. *Hurt people hurt people.*

Even if our parents and teachers taught us next to nothing about living solvent, we may have picked up some other nasty beliefs just by observing them. These may include: *Money causes fights in marriages;* or, *Men handle the money and always mess it up;* or, *Women are always overspenders.* Or, we may have acquired simple generalizations like *There's never enough money,* or *Money is always a problem.* I don't know anyone whose parents sat them down and said, "Here's how to assess what you will need; here's how to determine whether a job will offer enough to support you; here's how to do something you love and live within your means, even if you make less."

And in the end it doesn't matter. You're here now, with money trouble. The minute you get clarity with your own spending, all of the issues you picked up along the way will vaporize. You owe it to yourself and to those you love to learn how to live peacefully with your money. The good news is that you can be living debt-free within the first thirty days of working your Spending Plan. All of your relationships will benefit, and you can put your troubled money history to bed, for good.

THE ECONOMY, RECESSIONS, AND DEBT

Economic recessions can sweep us up in a financial hysteria and provide even more justification to act out around our money. For those of us with debt trouble, recessions can be a passport to what I call "gloom and doom debting." *The economy's in trouble, so I need to debt to live. I'm on a four-day week, so I need to debt to live. Everyone's having money trouble, so I need to debt to live.* Get the picture? Those of us who are debtors and have money trouble will use any excuse available to debt.

It's not that there are no real money concerns during a recession. It's not that people aren't really losing their jobs. They are. But if you get caught up in the hysteria, you'll miss the whole point of what you're trying to learn here: That if you live with financial clarity and within your means, a recession will not be able to frantically rock your world.

Can a recession devalue your home investment? Yes, it can. Can you lose your job? Yes, you can. But if you always live within your means, you will not lose your mind over a recession. You won't be debting against the equity in your house, should you own one. You will not be moving credit card debt around, nor will you accrue it, so you will not personally feel the pressure of a downturned economy, even if you lose a job. You will not spin into cycles of depression and anxiety over what you owe and now can't pay.

If you lose money investing, it will not be money you leveraged from your daily living expenses. In other words, no matter what happens, you will be solvent enough to face the changes that come rolling your way. And, take note, in my lifetime, there have been stock market dives, banking crises, and serious economic downturns about once every ten years. Recessions will come and they will go. But solvency—living debt-free—will always make the financial hailstorms that much easier to weather.

Pick Your Poison: What's Going to Stop You?

Most of us who have issues with money have some kind of anesthetic or addictive behavior, some kind of "tell" that lets us know we're trying to block what we can't deal with. I call it "The Sampler Plate of Checking Out." We spin the Sampler Plate and subconsciously ask ourselves, *What will I use today to absent myself from my money worries? Will it be overeating? Alcohol? Prescription drugs? Sex? Shopping? Overworking? Will I spiral into depression today and go dark on myself and my family? Will I beat myself up emotionally and then give up on myself?* These behaviors might not be severe enough to qualify us for professional help (or maybe they are), but they're intense enough to keep us *wallowing*, preventing us from taking steps toward change.

All of these—even the mood swings—are addictive patterns. We use them when we don't know what to do or how to proceed. We use them when we feel stuck. Our heart says we need to change something, but our mind can't figure out how, so we send our *will* into addictions. You've used these check-out tools before. And just because you're reading *The Debt-Free Spending Plan* doesn't mean you won't try to use them again. You probably will. In fact, reading this book is likely to trigger a compulsion or two.

So, identify your own addictive "tells," and make a simple attempt to interrupt them. Identify the things that you know you'll want to engage in instead of addressing your debt or spending. And even if you engage in the behavior, make an agreement with yourself right now that it won't stop you from reading and working the Debt-Free Spending Plan. Eventually, once you're working your Spending Plan, you won't need to check out, and the behaviors attached to your financial fear will likely fade and go.

"Checking out" means one thing and one thing only: You need help to change. *The Debt-Free Spending Plan* is here to help.

■　■　■

One last thought about personal roadblocks: *Please don't kill the messenger.* You may be thinking, *She doesn't have a clue how hard my situation is*, or *She uses too much kitschy language for me*, or *I don't see how she thinks a Debt-Free Spending Plan is going to help me*. Fine. Noted. And I'm going to invite you to set that aside and *get the message anyway*, regardless of my style or delivery.

We're debtors who don't like to look at our money issues. We're people without spending clarity who angst about it daily, and who will use just about any excuse to not directly address our money challenges. So I invite you to note your opinions and read on anyway. Have them, and work the Spending Plan anyway. You can still get the message even if you don't like the delivery.

So. Enough preamble. Let's see how *The Debt-Free Spending Plan* can work in your life.

2

. . . . .

In with Structure, Out with Stringency
The Simple Tools of the Debt-Free Spending Plan

HERE'S WHAT we're going to do to get started. We're going to create a simple Debt-Free Spending Plan just for you that will get you on track with your spending and help you stop debting forever. It will take you just five minutes a day to manage and it will include everything you'll need to live debt-free: (1) money for Bills and Daily Needs, (2) a Bill-Paying Plan, (3) a way to allocate money as it comes in, and (4) a plan to pay off debt without gouging your living expenses. And, it includes what's most important to all of us—money for projects we love, for fun, and for things that we want to experience. That's it. It's simple, easy, and clear.

Here's a promise: If you do the Debt-Free Spending Plan, you'll get free of debt pressures and you'll reclaim your life. Its simple structure will give you a foundation to keep you on track financially, with enough flexibility to deal with the usual glitches that show up in any given month.

The Spending Plan will ask you to add. It will ask you to subtract. It will ask you to write some things down. It will ask you to *be willing* to do something new. And for the price of a few minutes of your time each day, you'll get free of debt stress—now and forever. Sounds amazing, doesn't it? It is. So, let's get started.

First Things First: Determine Your Income

The first step in creating your Debt-Free Spending Plan is to make note of your income. Most of us will have some kind of job, but some of us won't. Some of us will have other sources of income, like alimony or unemployment insurance benefits. Whatever the source of your income is, take out a sheet of paper and write down the total amount you receive each month, or enter it on a blank computer document or in your financial software program. Then, write down how often you get paid.

This step may seem simplistic, but I've worked with debtors who were being cheated out of their wages because they and their bosses were unclear about how their salaries were calculated. For instance, one client had negotiated a rate of $17 an hour for her position as an assistant in a printing shop. She *and* her boss both calculated her salary by multiplying $17 times 80 hours—essentially, two weeks' worth of work. But, she was actually being paid twice a month. Since there are often more than ten working days in a half-month (for example, from July 15 to July 31, there are about twelve regular work days), she was being shorted for two to three days' worth of wages every month! This mistake cost her to lose a large chunk of income she had rightfully earned, and resulted in a hellish experience with her numbers-phobic boss trying to recover that money.

These are the kinds of situations that we tend to be vague about as debtors, especially when we shut down around numbers. So take a look. How much money do you *clear* every pay period? And, then, how often do you get paid?

WRITE IT DOWN

If you have no experience with a financial software package, but you can use a computer, then just use a Word document and create a list for each expense area. Or, if you're experienced in Excel or Quickbooks, or something similar, *and you like it*, use that program. You can use any app or program you choose, as long as you understand how to use it, easily and effortlessly.

Many of my clients start with a basic list of expenses in a Word document, learning the principles in the Debt-Free Spending Plan *first*, and then put the data into a different, more sophisticated program or format. If you're someone who shuts down around boxes, graphs, or math problems, don't panic. This plan makes it all as simple as possible, so just use what's easy for you—especially while you're learning. And never wait to learn a new software program before you start your Debt-Free Spending Plan.

ARE YOU UNDER-EARNING?

There are some people who are not earning what they need to live— not giving themselves reasonable amounts for rent, food, and medical care, let alone entertainment or money for fun. This goes back to our earlier premise about different kinds of money trouble. If you're a debtor, an overspender, a self-depriver, or even an "under-earner," you will still find help in the Debt-Free Spending Plan. Look at it this way: A healthy diet will help both the overweight person and the underweight person. Clarity will get you there, and clarity is what the Debt-Free Spending Plan is all about.

Over the past two decades, I've taught fund-raising classes to non-profit professionals—many of whom are under-earners and who work in organizations that also chronically "under-earn" and under-pay their professionals. It's a double whammy. But working for a cause doesn't have to mean a life of under-earning and debt. Nor does working less than full time or taking a job you love that pays less than you can earn elsewhere. The only way to assess whether or not you are truly under-earning is to create your personal Debt-Free Spending Plan. Then you compare what you have available for your needs with the actual costs of obtaining them. And then, regardless of your career path, you take action to earn a livable wage.

For now, what we're after is clarity in spending. If it becomes clear that you're not earning enough—maybe you're hanging out in a low-income, half-time job and not covering your expenses each month—then it will be that much easier for you to address your under-earning once you see your numbers written down. The Debt-Free Spending Plan is first and foremost a clarity tool. You get clarity first, and then you choose a right course of action for yourself.

IF YOU HAVE NO INCOME

If you have no income at all and you're living on credit cards or credit lines, I have only one tough-love thing to say to you: *Knock it off.* You and I both know it's a disastrous racket. I've done it myself several times in my life, and it only leads to pain and suffering. And it doesn't matter if you're doing it on the low end, covering a couple thousand dollars' worth of expenses, or on the high end, spending nine or ten thousand a month or more by borrowing against market-depleted real estate or running up your AmEx card. Just stop it! There's a moment when you agree with yourself to stop debting. Let this be the moment.

That said, each of us has to come to that "knock it off" moment in our own, good time. Sometimes it helps to ask yourself a simple question:

Is this as low as I have to go before I change, or do I have to fall lower?

Is this enough of a crash or does it have to be bigger?

In other words, *how big does your wakeup call have to be?* Is it going to be a stick? A 2-foot-thick beam that lands on your head? If you're debting just to live, you know the crash is coming. It's just the size of the crash that's in question.

So, if you need a job—go get one. If you have some savings and can live reasonably well on what you have (and you'll find that out when you craft your personal Debt-Free Spending Plan), then fine. For now. You can live on savings and a "downsized" Spending Plan for a while, but not forever. Under-earning is not your objective.

WHEN IT MAKES SENSE TO LIVE ON LESS

Yes, there are good reasons for people to live simply on less or on little income at certain times in their lives. But that works only if you have savings, or if you are easily covering your expenses on your lower income. Maybe you're dying to write that Himalayan trekking book and you're willing to downsize to do it. Maybe you want to start your own children's clothing line and you're willing to keep a half-time job and live frugally to do it.

The Debt-Free Spending Plan is a magical clarity tool for crafting and accomplishing your dreams. It will give you the clarity to know that you can live on less (and pass on a full-time day-job for a time) for a cause that's meaningful to you. But if you're living on credit, it doesn't matter *what* you're doing. You need a job and you need one right now.

Introducing the Debt-Free Spending Plan

The Debt-Free Spending Plan has three basic, simple components:

1. Monthly Bills

2. Daily Needs

3. Savings, Vacation, and Fun Money

If we get paid more than once a month, it will also have a Bill-Paying Plan. That's it. The premise is: We fund our bills (like mortgage or rent) and our daily needs (like groceries) first, and then we fund our savings, vacation, and "fun money."

This is what the basic structure of your Debt-Free Spending Plan will look like:

Income

July 6 paycheck	(	)
July 20 paycheck	(	)
Total	(	)
Necessities		
Bills (due monthly)	(	)
Daily Needs (food, fuel, etc.)	(	)
Totals	(	)
Balance	(	)
Savings, Vacation, and Fun Money	(	)

Take a moment and study the format. All of your "Necessities" are covered in two categories: Bills and Daily Needs. All it requires is that you add and subtract. The format is crafted around a simple question: *How much do you have, how much do you need, and what do you have left over?*

Now, at the beginning, for those of us who are in debt, we are not likely to have much left over after funding our Bills and Daily Needs. We may be making large credit-card payments or even overspending. Don't worry about that now. In a few short steps, we'll make changes that will impact our ability to *choose* what to spend and pay in each expense category—and *choosing* will free up some money in our "wants" and "needs" categories. For now, all we need to do is review the Debt-Free Spending Plan's categories and understand how the Spending Plan is set up.

So let's take a look at some typical Bills and Daily Needs categories.

THE DEBT-FREE SPENDING PLAN EXPENSE CATEGORIES

Note that the Spending Plan divides expenses into Bills and Daily Needs. Below is an example of how your expenses will be divided. Since each person's Spending Plan will be different, you may not need all of the categories listed here, or you may need to add a few. Keep in mind that the list of categories should be simple, so that it's easy to follow. If a category doesn't apply to you, you'll omit it from your Spending Plan. For now, just take a look at what the Spending Plan will cover.

<u>Bills</u>

Rent/Mortgage

Car Payment

Cell Phone

Phone/Internet

Health Insurance

Car Insurance

Child Care

Cable

Utilities

Gym

Newspaper Subscription

Movie Subscription

Monthly Dues

Automatic Savings

Credit Card 1

Credit Card 2

Bank Loan

Parent/Friend Loan Repayment

Daily Needs

Food (Groceries)

Fuel

Parking/Tolls/Public Transit

Medical Co-Pays

Drug Store

Beauty/Personal Care

Dry Cleaning

Laundry Home (coin-ops for apartments)

Household

Postage

Clothing

Haircut

Office Supplies

Entertainment

Children's Clothing

Children's Allowances

Children's Camps, Lessons, Soccer, etc.

Classes: Yoga, Arts, Sports, etc.

Massage/Acupuncture

Therapy

Cash Contributions

Almost everyone will need money for most of the items above in our categories list. You can easily add any categories you need that are not listed here, for items that are specific to your spending needs. In other words, the list of categories is personalized so it's just right for your expenses.

Step One: Your Monthly Bills

So, let's take a look at your first step toward achieving clarity—listing your monthly Bills. These Bills will include anything that's essentially a regular monthly payment. These items are all the fixed expenses that come around each and every month: things like rent, mortgage, health insurance, car payments, phone bills, utilities, and so on. They include your monthly gym expense, Netflix subscription, newspaper delivery, alimony, studio rent, monthly fees or dues, and any medical prescriptions that you must buy monthly. They do not include all prescriptions—just the ones that are regular monthly purchases, like birth control pills or daily cholesterol meds, for instance.

Think of it this way: "Bills" include anything that we are *required to pay* each month. They do *not* include dry cleaning, carwashes, haircuts, drug store items. These fall under the category of Daily Needs and are discussed in the next section. They are different from Bills because, at least theoretically, we can massage the amounts we spend on them.

Many of us who are debtors won't know the amounts of our monthly Bills or the dates they're due. So, do that footwork now. Check the due dates of your monthly bills and write in the actual amounts you're paying for each one on your personal Spending Plan. If you need to, call the companies who bill you and get the real numbers.

MAKE A LIST OF YOUR BILLS

Your next order of business in crafting your personal Debt-Free Spending Plan is to list each one of your bills, with its due date and the amount owed. Use the three columns listed below. It looks like this:

Bills	Due Date	Amount
Rent	1st	1,110.00
Car Payment	10th	394.00
Cell Phone	28th	80.00
Phone/Internet	7th	90.00

Additional bills as needed, until you list them all

The number in the "Amount" column is the total you think you'll need to cover the bill. It's just a simple list you're after here, so don't make it any more complicated than this example. Your Bills should remain basically the same every month. You won't have to change your amounts again unless your Bills go up or down (e.g., if your health insurance or rent increases, you'll have to make an adjustment).

Some bills may vary slightly. My monthly cell phone bill fluctuates between $76 to $80 (tax variances, 411 calls, etc.) each month. So, I plan for the largest amount I will ever spend, and then I list that amount on my own Debt-Free Spending Plan. (That way, I accrue a little extra money in my checking account each month— never a bad thing.)

If you're running up overage fees on your cell phone, randomly going over your minutes, you're going to gouge your Bills category very quickly. So, let me be clear: *You cannot go over your minutes and live debt-free.* If your cell phone plan is not adequate for your needs, change it. (We'll talk more about that in Chapter 5.)

The object is to have an extremely clear idea of what your Bills are each month, so you can reasonably plan to keep some money for yourself.

GET YOUR BILLS ARRANGED ON A MONTHLY CYCLE

In crafting your personal Debt-Free Spending Plan, you will be asked to make some changes in your Bills to make your life easier. One of these changes is to get your insurance payments (or other quarterly or bi-annual payments) switched to a *monthly debit system*, preferably with payments that come right out of your checking account. Most car, home, and renter's insurance companies offer a monthly billing option versus a six- or four-month billing cycle. Even if it costs you $2 or $4 more a month, make the change.

Why do we need to do this? Because we're debtors. We don't save for upcoming Bills—we don't even *think* about them most of the time, until they appear. That car insurance bill shows up six months later, and we stare at it as if it's a surprise, and then pay it with no plan, often depriving ourselves of Daily Needs money to do so—which only presses us to debt again. So we need *monthly amounts* to pay whenever possible; that way, we can be absolutely clear what it costs us to live each month.

In my own Debt-Free Spending Plan, the only nonmonthly payment I make is to the Department of Motor Vehicles, once a year, for my car registration. (We'll review how to deal with those nonmonthly expenses in Chapter 4.)

Look at it this way: If you have monthly accountability for *all* of your daily living expenses, then your income and savings can reasonably cover some of your wants, versus always having to cover "unexpected" and unplanned-for Bills.

Step Two: Your Daily Needs

Daily Needs are all the things you need to live day to day during any given month. They are the variable expenses that sustain you—your costs for food, clothing, household, and well-being expenditures.

If you've read a book or two (or more) on getting out of debt or on financial planning, you may have encountered a budget form that incorporates some of these categories. (It's quite surprising how many financial books *don't* offer a budget format or spending plan at all.) Most often, though, when a budget form is provided, the list of categories often gets so overwhelming that readers give up even before they begin. That's why I'm keeping this very, very simple—for me, for you, and for all of us who don't want to give up on ourselves this time. You're setting up a handful of categories to keep track of—and that's it. No Daily Needs list with forty-five headings and sixty-seven subcategories!

And why are you keeping your Bills list separate from your Daily Needs list? That's easy to explain. Because you *have to* pay your bills. Theoretically, your Daily Needs are flexible amounts—they're based on how much you have and how much you can spend. So, they're different from bills. You'll be able to massage them and adjust them more than you can your rent, for example. And that's exactly what you're going to do.

Let's do a little guesswork and ballpark your Daily Needs to get you started. We ballpark at first because what we spend on our Daily Needs is up to us, based on how much cash we have left over after paying our bills.

CREATE YOUR OWN DAILY NEEDS LIST

Give it a try. Use the following categories, and fill in the amounts you think you spend in one month.

Daily Needs	Amount
Food	
Fuel	
Parking/Tolls/Public Transit	
Medical Co-Pays	
Drug Store	
Beauty/Personal Care	
Dry Cleaning	
Laundry at Home (coin-ops for apartments)	
Household	
Postage	
Clothing	
Children's Clothing	
Haircut	
Office Supplies	
Entertainment	
Children's Allowances	
Children's Camps, Lessons, Soccer, etc.	

Classes: Yoga, Arts, Sports, etc.
Massage/Acupuncture
Therapy
Cash Contributions

Add any additional categories that are appropriate until you list them all

Step Three: Add It Up

First, add up your monthly income. Then add up your Bills and your ballparked Daily Needs expenses, and then add the totals of both categories. Use the example below as a guide:

Income

July 6 paycheck	$1,592.00 (net amounts, i.e., "cleared" cash)
July 20 paycheck	1,592.00
Total	$3,184.00

Necessities

Bills	$2,094.00
Daily Needs	1,350.00
Total	$3,444.00
Balance	**–$260.00**

Your expenses, as in the example above, probably outweigh your income. And, we haven't addressed the Savings, Vacation, or Fun Money component yet, right? But don't panic. This is what we expected. We're debtors. We overspend. The fact that we're spending more than we're bringing in should hardly surprise us.

So, don't freak out, and *don't give up*. You've barely begun to get yourself on track here. You *will* find ways to bring your spending into alignment with your income—and even free up some cash.

HOW TO MAKE THE NUMBERS WORK

Our lists of Bills and ballparked Daily Needs is our first wake-up call. There it is in black and white: We spend more than we make and *we've been adding credit card balances to our debting total*. So, our

Debt-Free Spending Plan comes into full play just where we might have guessed it would: with our Daily Needs. This is where the rubber meets the road.

If you clear $3,000 each month and your Bills total $2,000, then you can't spend more than $1,000 on your Daily Needs, including your Savings, Vacation, and Fun Money, and still stay solvent, can you? No. As debtors, we have to make our needs fit within what we have left after paying our bills. That's the bottom line.

That doesn't mean, though, that you won't take a look at how much your bills cost you and make some adjustments. And it doesn't mean you won't address credit card payments and how much they're eating into your money for monthly living expenses. You will. But right now—right out of the gate—you've got to make your Daily Needs fit within your income. That means you've got to cut. No B.S., if you plan to get free from debt and money stress, this is the moment that counts. You cut, and keep cutting until you make the numbers fit. That's the way it works.

For me, that meant allotting $250 a month for groceries instead of $800. That's about $62.50 a week! *Who can buy groceries on $62.50 a week and survive?* I thought. But I soon found out I could. When that's all I had, and that's all I could afford, and I was pledged to not debt, I did it. I stopped shopping at swanky, high-end, "whole paycheck" boutique groceries. I bought at the local ethnic supermarket where everything was half the price. I stopped feeding the neighborhood. I stopped hoarding and wasting food. I lived within my means. So, you can start now, too, and ballpark reasonable amounts that cover your real—and basic—needs. (A general rule of thumb: If money's tight, plan no more than $250 per person per month for groceries, and half of that for small children.)

If the real numbers for your Daily Needs are much lower than your first-pass numbers, tell yourself that this is your "downsized plan"—just a temporary plan to get you solvent and on to a more prosperous plan. Anyone can downsize for a little while.

THE SPENDING PLAN BUILDS SELF-RESPECT AND PRIDE
When you use the Debt-Free Spending Plan, you live within your means, and you build self-respect and pride. You find creative ways to get your needs met. You address your wants as well as your Bills and Daily Needs. You *plan* for things as simple as a paid-for vacation. You come back from the grocery store, the clothing store, and the weekend getaway with *no guilt* and with a sense of ease that you were able to give yourself and your family a nice experience without stressing over creating new debt for it.

THE PAY-OFF

You're probably saying to yourself right about now, *Just what's all of this going to get me? What's all this jockeying money around, balancing this against that going to do for me—really—in the end?* Fair questions.

What it's going to do is get you a paid-for vacation. It's going to get you a new shirt you love without any debtor's guilt. It's going to get you new tires when you need them, without any angst. It's going to fund holiday gifts with no credit card remorse. It's going to fund your art supplies or your trek up Kilimanjaro. It's going to get you clothing money, dentist money, shoe repair money, and dry cleaning money. It will give you movie money, dining money, and money for savings *every month*—all without the nasty little boxing match of voices fighting at fever pitches in your head. You know, the voices that holler:

"You know you shouldn't have bought that!"

"Oh shut up, will you? I needed that!"

"No, you didn't! You're only making things worse."

"I can't help it! I NEED things!"

"You're a total loser. You're never going to have any money if you keep running up debt!"

"SHUT UP! I CAN'T LISTEN TO YOU ANYMORE!"

"Well, you're going to have to listen, because you can't pay the damn mortgage!"

By making your monthly numbers work, you get to give up that head-ramming conversation for good. Forever.

And if all of that isn't reason enough, just remember that, as debtors, we're rebellious. Our debtor self does not like to be told what to do. It wants to overspend, and keep spending, even though it's killing us (and probably our families, too). So, if your adrenaline is ramping up for a fight just now, know that you're not alone. You're going to be resistant. So what. Be resistant and do the Debt-Free Spending Plan anyway. The payoff packs a punch your resistance has never seen the likes of.

DON'T CUT CATEGORIES

Don't cut any categories in your review of Daily Needs items. You can add categories as needed or craft combinations that are more useful to you, but make sure you don't eliminate them. In my current plan, I allocate $50 a month for vitamins and bodycare together, since I order them each month from a single online health food store. This allows me to cover both needs with one category and keeps my plan simple. To fund the new category, I simply adjusted my food and personal care categories down a bit and used those dollars for my new one.

Take special care not to cut categories for which you've had a tendency to debt. For instance, I hadn't ever planned for clothing expenses, and then I debted to fund all of them. For a lot of people, clothing is an easy category to dispense with. You may feel you're not a clothes horse, so what's the big deal, right? But, even if you've only got $10 a month for clothing (or whichever category you're anxious to cut), *keep it in there*. If you don't use the category one month, then stick the cash in an envelope and save it for the day you need a new coat or you've got to rent a tux. Everyone needs new sneakers, new boots, and new underwear from time to time. Stash it or spend it, but don't cut it.

The message here is this: Cutting categories breeds deprivation, and deprivation breeds debt. And you don't want to get on that merry-go-round anymore.

The One, Hard-and-Fast Rule

Here's the one, big rule for doing the Debt-Free Spending Plan. *Cut your Daily Needs enough to have some money left for Savings, Vacation, and Fun.* I don't care if it's $5 in each category. When I was totally broke, and just starting a lower paying job, my Debt-Free Spending Plan had exactly $5 a month in each of these three categories. As we get healthier financially, we're able to put more cash toward each of these priorities. For now, though, you're just starting to do that.

To begin, open a (free) savings account each for Savings and Vacation, and put your Fun Money in an envelope for the month so you have money for something pleasurable to look forward to. At this point, it's all more about the consciousness of setting money aside than the actual amounts you set aside. If you can afford to put $100 in each category—or more—by all means, do it. The objective is to reasonably fund your Bills and Daily Needs, and then make the rest of your money *work for what's meaningful to you.*

Also, don't skip the Entertainment category in your Daily Needs list. Once again, even if it's $5 a month, keep it in there. Entertainment (aka, rest and relaxation) is a genuine human need and we need to fund it. At first, my Debt-Free Spending Plan was so close to the bone that I had only $2 in my Entertainment category. Within a year, though, I had $100 a month to spend. It's an amazingly simple joy to give ourselves the gift of relaxation. It breeds ease and well-being, and it makes us feel good about what we're providing for ourselves and our families. So, start funding Entertainment now, even if it's a very small amount.

YOUR SAVINGS, VACATION, AND FUN MONEY

The best part about learning to live debt-free is that we finally—and mercifully—stop living with debt pressures. But there's another silver lining. We also start building our dreams. We begin setting aside money for vacations, projects, long-term goals—and for *fun*. By creating money clarity in our lives, we stop unaccountable spending, and that's amazing all by itself. But that clarity supports something even more incredible: *When we live within our means we have money for the things we truly want and love*. The importance of this part of the Debt-Free Spending Plan cannot be underestimated. That's why I have dedicated an entire chapter to the subject (Chapter 4). For now, we're going to continue learning the Spending Plan's outline, and soon enough we'll address dream building in detail.

■ ■ ■

Now, let's move on to Chapter 3, where I will show you how to put the Debt-Free Spending Plan into action.

3

· · · · ·

Make It Work Every Day

Your Personal Debt-Free Spending Plan in Action

IN THE LAST chapter, I introduced the Debt-Free Spending Plan, and we learned the basics of how it works. So, let's put it all together and view an example that takes us further. Note that no matter what your income, you must make the numbers balance. When you do that—when you live within your means—the amounts you spend in each category will be reasonable and proportional in relation to your income.

A Typical Debt-Free Spending Plan

Here's a completed example of a Debt-Free Spending Plan. Note that we're using the same example as we showed in the last chapter, only this time we're going to make the numbers balance. In the first pass, in Chapter 2, my example showed that I was over my cash income by $260. But by doing some simple downsizing, I was able to free up cash for meaningful savings, fun, and entertainment—as well as balance my Spending Plan.

Summary

Income

July 6 paycheck	$1,592.00
July 20 paycheck	1,592.00
Total	$3,184.00

Necessities

Bills	$2,094.00
Daily Needs	914.00
Total	$3,008.00

Balance

$3,184.00 (Income)
−3,008.00 (Necessities)
=$176.00 (Left over)

Fun, Savings, Vacation	+176.00
Fun (spend on anything I like)	50.00
Savings Account	80.00
Vacation Account	46.00
Total	176.00

Monthly Plan Detail

Bills	Due Date	Amount
Rent	1st	1,110.00
Car Payment	28th	394.00
Cell Phone	21st	80.00
Phone/Internet	7th	90.00
Health Insurance	10th	45.00 (my contribution)
Car Insurance	10th	91.50

Cable	N/A	N/A
Utilities	25th	25.00
Gym	7th	27.00
Newspaper Subscription	N/A	N/A
Movie Subscription	21st	8.00
Monthly Dues	N/A	N/A
Automatic Savings	10th	25.00
Credit card 1	27th	45.00 min
Credit card 2	25th	67.00 min
Bank Loan	28th	86.50 min
Parent Loan Repayment	[Not paying yet]	
Total		2,094.00

Daily Needs	Amount
Food (groceries)	250.00
Fuel	225.00
Parking/Tolls/Public Transit	10.00
Medical Co-pays	30.00
Drug Store	25.00
Beauty/Personal Care	25.00
Dry Cleaning	30.00
Laundry at Home (coin-ops for apartments)	20.00
Household	25.00
Postage	9.00
Clothing	60.00
Haircut	40.00
Office Supplies	10.00
Entertainment	20.00
Yoga	100.00
Cash Contributions	35.00
Total	914.00

Your Spending Plan will look just like this, only it will cover your specific needs and any category additions that are particular to your spending. This is what you're going to do each and every month—

that is, plan out your income and your expenditures *before you spend one dime*. This is the beginning of your financial ease and peace of mind with your money.

A Quick Emotional Read on the Numbers

Before we learn how to work the Spending Plan in a daily way, let's get an emotional read on the numbers in this example. You may be in the same income category as the example (or somewhere near it), and be panicking about now. *There's no cable in this Spending Plan! There's almost no dining-out money! There's only $25 in beauty/personal care! What about my waxing? What about my $75 weekend round of golf? What about my morning $3.50 latte every day?*

If you can make those expenses work in your Spending Plan without depriving yourself elsewhere and *without debting*, then be my guest. If you can't, then you have to find another way to fund those needs—or cut them. End of story. The amounts in your Daily Needs categories will be *proportional to the amount you have left over after paying your bills*. In other words, you've got to make the numbers work for *all* of your needs. You can't gouge in one or two areas and expect to stay solvent.

In the example, there's no room for $105 for lattes every day ($3.50 × 30 days) unless I reduce some Bills or cut more Daily Needs. I could exchange yoga for coffee—but that's not a really great choice if the yoga keeps me fit, is it? I can't very well cut food by $105 a month—I'm living pretty simply at $250 a month as it is, right? I could, however, use some of my Fun Money ($50) for coffees, if that's how I'd like to spend it. Or I could get a cheap gym membership that offers yoga and allot the rest to Fun Money or a coffee fund.

Here's another example: $300 a month for four rounds of weekend golf ($75 × 4 weekends) just isn't going to work in this Spending Plan because I wouldn't have enough for food and fuel. But, since a round of golf costs me $75, I could use my $50 of Fun Money and downsize my Spending Plan by $25 to play golf once a month, couldn't I?

Get it? Looking at the numbers straight up will make you assess larger issues about what's most important to you. So, if you're living debt-free for the first time and you're on a downsized Spending Plan, do you really want to be spending more than $100 a month on *coffee*? On *lunches out*? On *waxing*? Isn't there something more meaningful you'd like to have—like a vacation, a new ten-speed, a buffer in the bank, a romantic dinner out, or cash for the holidays? How about buying a coffee maker and a bag of gourmet beans, and making your own for a while? How about canceling the cable and renting movies for free from the library or streaming them off the Internet for a while? It won't kill you.

The bottom line is that you've got to make the numbers work, solvent and debt-free. I'm not going to tell you what you can and can't have. You've got some cash to fund your Daily Needs, and you've got some Fun Money. You get to choose what's most important to you. If it's the coffee over the yoga, then fine. If it's the cable over the gym, that's your choice. But you have to do it all on what you earn, and you have to cover *all* of your needs. Period.

Do Your Plan Once a Month, Every Month

Do your Debt-Free Spending Plan each month by about the 28th. Don't dawdle, and don't drag your feet—because you're not going to spend one damn dime until you have your Spending Plan. At first it's going to take you a couple of hours to get it done. If nothing much changes in your income, everything will stay about the same for subsequent months. If fuel costs go up or your health insurance premium increases, you'll have to make some adjustments before a new month begins. Once again, it's simple addition and subtraction we're talking about here. Anyone can do it.

Though it's simple to do, it is going to take a while to get used to working your Spending Plan. It'll feel cumbersome at first. You won't be used to writing things down. That's okay. That's normal. Though you'll be living debt-free within the first month of using your Spending Plan, it'll probably take until the third month to feel completely relaxed with it. Be patient. By the sixth month, it will be so ingrained that you won't be able to think about starting the month without it.

Simply put, the Debt-Free Spending Plan is what puts you on the map financially—it's a path-by-path roadway that gets you where you want to go. And where do you want to go exactly? You want to pay your bills (on time), you want to fund your living expenses (with ease), and you want to plan for something that's meaningful to you. That's it.

When we live without a Spending Plan, we overspend in some areas and deprive ourselves in other areas. We spend $250 on over-priced vitamins and don't have enough for food or medical co-pays. We blow more than we can possibly eat at the grocery store or the bulk warehouse, and then debt to fund new tires. We're out of control and without accountability when we're without a Spending Plan. We need the structure of knowing what to spend our money on, and how much we can spend in each category, *so that we have something left over for ourselves.* That's the only way it's going to happen. Winging it has just brought us headaches and heartaches. So, from now on, make a Spending Plan every month—from now until the day you die.

The Magic Little Notebook

The first tool in your debt-free toolbox is your Debt-Free Spending Plan. The second tool is the Magic Little Notebook. Here's how it works.

Go to your local drug or sundries store and pick up a 3 x 5-inch notebook. It'll cost less than $2. Now, open the notebook and write your list of Daily Needs in it, including each monthly amount and giving each category a page or two. "Food $250" on one page, "Fuel $225" on another page, "Medical co-pays $30" on another, and so on. Food and fuel, the items that will have the most activity, will probably need at least two pages of your notebook. Write all the amounts that are in your Daily Needs list in your notebook, page by page. You don't need to do this with your Bills—just your Daily Needs.

Now, here's where the Debt-Free Spending Plan differs from all the other financial advice you've read before now. Once you've done your Spending Plan each month, and have made the numbers fit, you need a way to *work* the Spending Plan in a daily way. You can't just list monthly amounts for each category and *hope* you stay within them. We're all debtors. We hate numbers. We don't like paying attention to how much money we spend. So, we need a simple tool to help us do that—something so basic that we can't screw it up, or throw up our hands and say, "It's too complicated!" and give up.

The Magic Little Notebook is that tool. It will keep you solvent each and every month. *If you do nothing else besides plan your expenses and use your Magic Little Notebook, you will always stay solvent.* It works like this. You go to the gas station, use your debit card, and put $27.35 in your tank. The first thing you do when your butt hits the car seat (or when you get home, or first thing in the morning) is write that amount in your Magic Little Notebook. This is how it looks:

Fuel	225.00
7/6 Eagle Gas Station	−$27.35
	+197.65

The next time you gas up, you do the same thing, writing the amount you spent in your notebook, just like the example below.

Fuel	225.00
7/6 Eagle Gas Station	−$27.35
	+197.65
7/14 Chevron Gas Station	−$33.12
	+164.53

Each time, you subtract the amount you have spent, so that you see what you have left. Always use + or − signs in front of the numbers so you don't mix up what you have and what you're subtracting. Carry your Magic Little Notebook with you everywhere you go, and *look in your book before you buy anything.* Make sure you have the money *before* you spend it.

Spend only what you need for that week. For food and fuel, ballpark what you have for each week and spend only that amount. *Don't even dream that you're going to "stock up" for the month.* Get in the habit now of ridding yourself of hoarding behavior. You can't afford it and it's not healthy, anyway. If you've got $250 for groceries and there are five Saturdays in the month, shop on weekends and spend $50 a week for groceries. If there are four Saturdays, you've got $62.50.

OVERAGES AND NORMAL HUMAN ERROR

Here's the beauty of the Magic Little Notebook. Let's say you've got $30 a month for dry cleaning, and when you go to pick up your clothes, the clerk says, "That's going to be $35, please." You don't have to panic and leave your clothes at the cleaners for another month. You can use the notebook to keep yourself solvent between categories as well as within them.

So, if I go over $5 in dry cleaning, can I take $5 from the household category this month? Do I have any big purchases coming up for the house? If not, move $5 from household to dry cleaning, and even the expense out. *Write the money move down in each category. Don't skip this part.* Later, when you need to refer back to what you spent in household, you'll be able to follow the money trail. It looks like this:

On one page:

Dry Cleaning	30.00
7/10 A-1 Cleaners	−$35.00
	−$5.00

7/10 From Household	+$5.00
	$0

And, on another page:

Household	20.00
7/3 Walgreens–kitchen stuff	−$7.23
	+$12.77
7/10 To Dry Cleaning	−$5.00
	+$7.77

Here's a general rule of thumb: You'll be tempted to do a lot of money moves from food and fuel because they're the largest categories. Don't do it—or do it very sparingly. When you're on a downsized plan, food and fuel are the expense items you'll most need to guard, since you'll consistently need both of them all the way through the month.

If you have leftover money at the end of the month—say you didn't use your $20 in household money—*and your income is stable*, then use it for whatever you like. You can spend it or you can pay it forward to next month's expenses, giving you more Savings, Vacation, or Fun Money for the new month. The premise of this Spending Plan is that there will always be new money for household and dry cleaners and clothes—for all your needs—every month. So if you spend or stash any small amounts of leftover cash, it's not going to hurt you. It's a just reward for living within your means.

THE NOTEBOOK'S OBJECTIVE

You might be thinking, *This seems like a royal pain in the behind— what's all this writing-down-my-numbers going to get me, really?* Your payoff for working your Magic Little Notebook is simple: *You get to keep some money for yourself.* Vacation money. Fun Money. Savings and Entertainment money. On the other hand, every time you spend mindlessly, racking up expenses with no plan and no accountability, *you steal money from yourself.* That's right.

By spending without a Spending Plan, or going over without accounting for it, we steal money from the things that would have been more meaningful to us than stocking up on paper towels or carting home six containers of ten-pack chicken breasts. Get it? When you use the Magic Little Notebook to stay within the amounts you have set down at the beginning of the month: *you will always get to keep the money you set aside for your wants.* That's kind of a revelation, isn't it?

TRACKING YOUR EXPENSES: WHY BOTHER?

The truth is, if all you ever do is map out your monthly Debt-Free Spending Plan, pay your bills, and live by the amounts listed in your Magic Little Notebook, you will always, always be solvent. So why track your numbers at all? Why do the extra work of having a list of expenditures?

Because it shows us *trends* in our spending and gives us ridiculously easy tax information at the end of the year. Trends show us if we need to increase or decrease spending in specific categories, or they tell us if we're truly under-earning. If we're a consultant, home office professional, entrepreneur, or an artist of any kind and need to list deductions on our tax returns, tracking our expenses saves us a lot of money. And, should we ever need to figure out when we paid for those car repairs, or what warranty is still good based on its purchase date, or which month we'll find the receipt for the now-broken DVD player, it'll all be right there in our tracking record.

Your Personal Tracking Record

Before I created the Debt-Free Spending Plan, I had an accountant set up all of my expenditure categories in Quickbooks. I didn't know how to use the software very well (beyond entering my receipts), and

I was intimidated by it and had no extra money to pay someone to teach me how to use it. Honestly, I just didn't like it and I felt like I was screwing up each time I used it. Finally I just stopped entering my numbers altogether and gave up.

Before the Quickbooks experience, I used to stuff all of my yearly receipts into large brown envelopes and then spent four unbearable, fifteen-hour days at the end of each year sorting them and adding them up. It was an angst-producing, drama-inducing activity that I moaned about to anyone who would listen. Today, with my Spending Plan, my tax worksheet for the year takes me exactly two hours. That's it. How come? Because I track every expenditure I make in a simple list on my Debt-Free Spending Plan.

Tracking is simple. You list your Daily Needs expenses on the same document page as your Debt-Free Spending Plan. Or you use graph paper and write down the expenses in each category by hand. Or you use a program like Quicken, Quickbooks, or your banking software, or an app to track your expenditures—*but only if you love using it and know how to use it well*. It doesn't matter what you use. Again, the rule here is to use whatever you know and to start now: Do not wait until you learn a new software program.

The simplest way I've found to track my numbers is to copy my Daily Needs list in my Spending Plan and list what I spend. It looks like this:

Daily Needs

Food	250.00
7/8 Trader Joe's	35.19
7/9 Dean's Produce	23.19
7/15 Marina Market	29.17
7/16 Mollie Stone's	4.50
7/17 Trader Joe's	25.33
Fuel	225.00
7/7 Union 76	44.19
7/16 Eagle Gas	45.12

Parking/Tolls/Public Transit	10.00
7/16 Bridge toll	4.00

Medical Co-pays	30.00
7/10 Dr. Hughes	15.00

A very simple list is all you really need. If you're using a computer program or an app, set up your Debt-Free Spending Plan categories inside it and the program will automatically add up your totals each month. If you're using a simple list in a Word document, it takes about five minutes to add up your numbers at the end of each month. (Many banks also have expenditure-tracking software available for their clients' use for a small fee.)

An important note: The tracking record is an objective report of what you have spent. It's a list of where the actual dollars went. If you moved $30 from dry cleaning to food in your Magic Little Notebook to cover a dinner party, your month-end tracking totals will reflect that. Dry cleaning will have $0 and food will have about $30 more in expenses. Your Magic Little Notebook keeps you within the overall totals you set out at the beginning of the month, and your tracking record tells you what you actually spent in each category. But you don't have to replicate the money moves you used in your Magic Little Notebook. All you do on your tracking record is list where the money actually got spent.

RECEIPTS, TIME, AND MONEY

So, when do you do your tracking? Once a day. Pick a time and do it every day at the same time. Here's what I do: Every morning I dig out all of my receipts from the day before and I write them down in (1) my Magic Little Notebook (if I haven't already noted them), (2) my checkbook, and (3) my tracking record. Like I said, it takes five minutes.

My husband carries his Magic Little Notebook in his work satchel or his car. I carry mine in my purse or a bag. He likes to wad all of his receipts in his pockets and throw them on the table when he gets home, unraveling them as he enters them in his notebook, checkbook, and tracking record. I like to keep my receipts in a side pocket of my purse and enter them in my notebook the minute my butt hits the car seat. Then I do my tracking record and checkbook first thing in the morning.

It doesn't matter how you do it—just that you do it every day. It takes me five minutes most days, maybe seven or eight during the holidays when I'm purchasing more. Five minutes a day to get free. That's it.

What about weekends off? What about vacations? you ask. *I don't want to have to do this every day!* And I say, fine. Do it anyway. The object is to have your Magic Little Notebook with you wherever you go and whenever you spend. And then, once a day, you record what you have spent. You won't spend any money without looking to see if you have the cash, and you'll always keep track of what you're spending. That way, all month long you can sashay out the door with your debit card and your Magic Little Notebook and know you'll always stay solvent.

STASH RECEIPTS BY THE MONTH

So, what do you do with all of those receipts? I stash all of my receipts for the month in a regular or mid-size envelope, label it by month, and when the month is over, I put the envelope someplace safe. That way, January's receipts are always in one place and always match January's Debt-Free Spending Plan. If I have to go back and dig up a receipt for any reason, I can quickly check my recent Spending Plans to find where it's listed, and then go straight to the right envelope. It takes me less than five minutes. All of my numbers will be on my tracking record, so there's never a need to tediously sort receipts at the end of the tax year. It's already done.

**TRACKING FOR CONSULTANTS, HOME OFFICE
PROFESSIONALS, ENTREPRENEURS, AND ARTISTS**

If your business is a sole proprietorship, and your business expenses
come out of your Daily Needs spending, then use the following form
for your tracking record. (This is most useful for keeping track of
Schedule C tax deductions.)

Food	250.00	Business Expense
7/8 Trader Joe's	35.19	
7/9 Dean's Produce		23.19 Cooked business lunch
7/15 Marina Market	29.17	
7/16 Molly Stone's	7.50	
7/17 Trader Joe's	25.33	
Fuel	225.00	Business Expense*
7/7 Union 76	44.19	*tracked by mileage
7/16 Eagle Gas	45.12	
Parking/Tolls/Public Transit	10.00	Business Expense
7/16 Bridge toll		4.00 J. Ansell meeting
Medical Co-pays	30.00	Business Expense
7/10 Dr. Hughes	15.00	
Drug Store	25.00	Business Expense
7/15 Walgreens (split: 11.32 total)	8.33	2.99 business envelopes
Office Supplies	20.00	Business Expense
7/2 Office Depot paper		11.79

Get it? Just use your existing Debt-Free Spending Plan numbers
and separate the expenses into business and personal columns. It's
that easy. If you run expenses through a separate business checking
account, then create a Debt-Free Spending Plan specifically for your
business account and expenses.

Your Bill-Paying Plan

So far, your toolbox includes a Debt-Free Spending Plan, a Magic Little Notebook, and a Tracking Record. If you get paid once a month—let's say on June 28 or on July 1 for July's expenses—then the Debt-Free Spending Plan needs no extra instructions. You won't need a detailed Bill-Paying Plan because you'll pay your bills once a month, the same way as they're listed in your plan. However, if you get paid every two weeks, you'll need another strategy to help you allocate your monthly income as it comes in. It's called a Bill-Paying Plan, and it's explained below. But, first, let's discuss paying your bills with a once-a-month paycheck.

BILL PAYING ON A MONTHLY PAYCHECK

Here's what you'll do if you get one paycheck per month. You'll put your paycheck into your checking account, pay your Bills, and fund your Savings, Vacation, and Fun Money categories. (Once again, we'll talk more about allocating money for savings in Chapter 4.) Then you'll fund your Daily Needs (all month long), drawing from your checking account in accordance with your Debt-Free Spending Plan. You'll use your Magic Little Notebook and debit card to keep yourself solvent each time you make a purchase. If you have a tendency not to allow yourself any Entertainment or Fun Money, you'll take that money out in cash and put it in a labeled envelope. That way you can't be tempted to spend it on a bill.

Here's a note to consultants: You must get your monthly checks on time. That means you've got to invoice your clients by the previous month or mid-month to get your check by the first of the following month. Piecing together your living-expense money throughout the month will only confuse you and undermine your efforts. So, get your clients on the same schedule as you're on. If you have trouble invoicing, get support. Mark your invoicing dates on your calendar and set up an "accountability call" with someone you trust who will hold you to your due date. Sabotaging your money by not invoicing or repeatedly allowing yourself to be paid late is drama seeking. (If you have this challenge, attend a support group where you can get solid help.)

BILL-PAYING ON A TWO-WEEK PAYCHECK

What if you don't get paid monthly? Most of us get paid every two weeks—and that confuses things a bit, since we're not getting paid on the first of the month, right? This is where most financial books fell down the chute for me. The few books that did offer a monthly budget or spending plan didn't offer any guidance on how to use that budget or plan—and that wasn't enough for a debtor who shuts down around her numbers. What I needed was a specific Bill-Paying Plan to help me fund my expenses based on when I got paid.

If you get paid every two weeks or bi-monthly (on the 15th and the 30th), you've got to have a Spending Plan that lets you know when to pay each bill. Why is this important? Because if your money is close to the bone, you're not going to have a stash of cash lying around that will immediately get you paid up on your bills so you can start ahead of the curve. You're probably living paycheck to paycheck, right? So how do you do it?

First, map the dates your paychecks will come in. (Use automatic deposit if your employer offers it, since you will have quicker access to your cash. We're all going to give up the angst of rushing to the bank to cover overdue bills.) So, let's say, as our example illustrates, you get paid on July 6 and July 20, and you're clearing $1,592 each pay period. In a perfect world, you would have paid your rent out of your last June paycheck—that is, the June 21 paycheck will cover the July 1 rent due date. In that case, your Bill-Paying Plan would look like this:

Bill-Paying Plan

July 6 Check	Due Date	1,592.00
Daily Needs		914.00
Savings, Vacation, Fun		176.00

Cell Phone	21st	80.00
Phone/Internet	7th	90.00
Health Insurance	10th	45.00 (my contribution)
Car Insurance	10th	91.50
Utilities	25th	25.00
Gym	7th	27.00
Automatic Savings	10th	25.00
Credit card 1	27th	45.00 min
Credit card 2	25th	67.00 min
Total		1,585.50

Leaves +6.50 in checking

July 20 Check	**Due Date**	**1,592.00**
		+6.50 (leftover from July 6 check)
		=1,598.50
Rent for August	1st Aug	1,110.00
Car Payment	28th	394.00
Bank Loan	28th	86.50 min
Movie Subscription	21st	8.00
Total		1,598.50

Exactly even

Notice that if you get paid every two weeks your *Debt-Free Spending Plan will not begin on the first of the month.* It will begin with your first paycheck deposit of the month. So your Magic Little Notebook numbers—your Daily Needs expenses—begin, in this example, on July 6. You won't pre-spend a damn thing. Your July money kicks in when you get it, and not one millisecond beforehand.

This also means that your July Daily Needs money will roll over into August—in this case, through August 3, when you get paid again. *Your Daily Needs money for the month always kicks in with the first paycheck of the month.*

Note that several of the bills covered by the July 6 check are not due until later in the month. Pay them when you get your check anyway, or as soon as you get the bill in the mail. Let the July 6 paycheck cover all of the listed bills in your Bill-Paying Plan for that check—and *no more than that.* Don't pay any other bills in your excitement over your newfound solvency or you'll blow your whole Spending Plan.

Work it out so that your bills and your automatic deductions are covered on the dates they're due. If you have too much coming out of your account in one pay period, call your service provider and get your billing cycle changed so it works for you. In general, *always pay a little ahead wherever you can, but don't deprive yourself to do it.*

Now, here's the big caveat. We always want to fund all of our Daily Needs in the first paycheck of the month, if at all possible. Why? Because we've all got issues with numbers, and if we try to piece together parts of our Daily Needs expenses, we're likely to confuse ourselves and give up. We don't want that! We're after clarity here. So, fund what you need to live right away. It'll give you a sense of security and ease to know that all of your Daily Needs are covered and written down in your Magic Little Notebook at the beginning of the month. If you can't do it at first, that's okay. You'll get there.

YES, IT'S WORTH THE EFFORT

Does creating a Bill-Paying Plan seem like a lot of extra work? Are you wriggling in your chair right now, thinking, *I shouldn't have to do that!* Or, *That's just way too much effort!* If so, then just remember: we're all debtors. We get a rush from the adrenaline that comes from being confused about our bills.

So, if you feel resistant to making a Bill-Paying Plan, that's good. It's normal. Do it anyway. You'll only have to do it once, and after that, you'll know what to pay with each and every paycheck. No more confusion. No more late dates or fees. And guess what? Without all that swirling, panicky energy in your bill-paying cycles, you can actually give your attention to something (or someone) you're interested in!

What to Do if You're Behind

Many of us debtors have been behind in our bill paying, so paying our July rent from our June paycheck might just be a lovely pipe dream. Even if that's the case, don't give up. It'll take a little bit of extra mapping, that's all. If you're behind and paying your rent with your July 6 check, your Bill-Paying Plan looks like this:

July 6 Check	Due Date	1,592.00
Rent for July	1st	1,110.00
Daily Needs	= ½ of 914.00	457.00
Automatic Savings	10th	25.00
		1,592.00 Exactly

July 20 Check	Due Date	1,592.00
Daily Needs	= ½ of 914.00	457.00
Savings, Vacation, Fun		176.00
Cell Phone	21st	80.00
Phone/Internet	7th	90.00
Health Insurance	10th	45.00 (my contribution)
Car Insurance	10th	91.50
Utilities	25th	25.00
Gym	10th	27.00
Credit card 1	27th	45.00 min
Credit card 2	25th	67.00 min
Car Payment	28th	394.00
Bank Loan	28th	86.50 min
Movie Subscription	21st	8.00
Total		1,592.00 Exactly

The first thing to note here is that several bills get paid late, since the rent is getting paid late. No worries. Just do what you need to do. Call your providers and let them know, and try to change the cycle to fit your needs. If it means putting your gym membership on hold for a month, skipping the movie subscription, or decreasing your Savings, Vacation, and Fun Money until you catch up, then do it.

Do the best you can to downsize your plan until you're on track again—until your monthly cash covers all of your expenses in a timely way. You have Daily Needs (like food and fuel) all month long, and you need to fund them, so it's *not* your objective to deprive yourself for half the month for these needs so you can pay bills. Your best bet is to adjust the due dates to fit your Debt-Free Spending Plan or do your best to pay bills as close to on time as possible.

Once again, to make this Bill-Paying Plan work, you cannot begin spending your Daily Needs money until July 6, because that's when this Bill-Paying Plan begins. You are so close (no extra) here with your dollars that it's absolutely imperative that you get this: Your $457 for two weeks of Daily Needs does not kick in until July 6, *when you get your money.* Don't pre-spend a damn thing—because you don't have the cash yet.

And, since you can't fund all of your Daily Needs at the beginning of the month, you'll write down *half* of what your Spending Plan says in your Magic Little Notebook. On July 20, when you get your next paycheck, you'll write new pages and list the other half of your Daily Needs. The principle is simple: We don't spend it until we have it.

Here's how this looks in your Magic Little Notebook:

On the first page:

Food—July 6–20   125.00 (½ of 250.00)

On the next page:

Fuel—July 6–20   112.50 (½ of 225.00)

On the next page:

Parking/Tolls/Public Transit—July 6–20   5.00 (½ of 10.00)

Got it? You're listing one-half of what you put in your monthly Debt-Free Spending Plan for Daily Needs, because you can only fund half of your expenses at a time. This system also means that your July 20 Daily Needs money will roll over into the next month. Your July 20 paycheck will cover your Daily Needs until August 3, or whenever your next paycheck arrives. *Once again, we fund our needs based on when our cash comes in.*

How to Catch Up

Now, here's how to use the Spending Plan to catch up and start paying your bills ahead of schedule. Two to four times a year, on an every two-week paycheck schedule, you'll get an extra check (because there will be three paydays in the month). Use that third paycheck to get ahead.

First, give yourself half of your monthly Spending Plan's Daily Needs and put the numbers in your Magic Little Notebook. This will cover your needs for the next two weeks. Then, use the rest of the cash to pay ahead on your bills (your rent or mortgage, especially). Start your new month's Debt-Free Spending Plan with your next check. You'll be caught up for the rest of the year. Sound confusing? It's not, really. What all this means is simple: *Allocate your money.* Make sure you have enough to cover your Daily Needs and Bills, based not just on monthly amounts but also on when your cash comes in.

STAYING SOLVENT

The only way you're going to stay solvent is by having a Debt-Free Spending Plan that's as clear as one, two, three:

1. How much do you have?

2. When does it come in?

3. What can you spend, and when?

Extreme clarity—that's what we're after here. That's the only thing that helps us make peace with our money.

What to Do if You're Ahead

Most of us won't have to worry right away about what to do if we're ahead in our bill paying. But by working the Debt-Free Spending Plan, many of us will end up being ahead of the due-date game. So what do we do when we're allocating June's paychecks for July's expenses, and we haven't even gotten our bill statements in the mail yet? Do we just leave a month or two of extra expense cash in our checking account?

No, we don't. How come? Because we're debtors. And when it looks like we have "extra" money sitting around, we tend to get crazy and do irresponsible things—like spend it all on stuff we really don't need and really can't afford. Your Debt-Free Spending Plan will tell you what you can spend and what you can't. And since you're the one who's creating your Spending Plan every month anyway, if there's enough extra to buy something you really love, you can *plan* to buy it. But put everything in your Spending Plan first. Then you get to have all the joy of your purchase without any debtor's regret.

So, let's say all of your June bills are paid; all of your Daily Needs money for the month is in your checking account; your Savings, Vacation, and Fun Money is funded—and you still have two more June paychecks coming in. What do you do?

This is what you do. You set up a savings account and nickname it your "Healthy Reserve" account. You put *all* of your paychecks into your Healthy Reserve account as they come in. By the first of each month, you withdraw *the exact amount of cash you will need* to cover your Debt-Free Spending Plan for the upcoming month. You put it into your checking account. (Connect your Healthy Reserve account to your checking account for easy online transfers, or make a bank visit at the first of the month to transfer the cash.)

In this setup, you will always accrue your paycheck overages in your Healthy Reserve account—and that account will grow as you earn. Your ultimate goal is to set aside three months of living expenses in this account, which will insulate you from recessions, economic downturns, job losses, and feeling like you "have to" stay in a dysfunctional job setting. Always having three months of living expense money in a Healthy Reserve account helps you relax, and when you're relaxed, you're easier to work with, easier to live with, and easier to be around in general.

The Healthy Reserve account is not a short-term slush fund. (We'll talk about productive long- and short-term savings in Chapter 4.) This reserve account is holy. It's a sacred chunk of cash that allows you the dignity of no-panic when the earth shifts under your feet. In other words, don't touch the overages in your Healthy Reserve account for anything less than a major financial crisis. When a crisis strikes, as it inevitably will, you won't be one of the hand-wringing, hair-pulling masses. You've got yourself a reserve.

"Payday Debting": Consultants, Home Office Professionals, Entrepreneurs, and Artists

Reserve accounts are particularly important for consultants, home office professionals, entrepreneurs, and artists. In fact, they're critical. Why? Because when we work for ourselves, we don't get paid on a regular schedule and need to plan for the months when there is no paycheck.

Consultants, entrepreneurs, and artists are especially famous for "payday debting." That's when we get that big $6,000 or $12,000 end-of-project check and we go crazy spending as if we were getting paid this way every month. We know this money's got to last us until the next client pays (and we often don't even have another client yet), but we get money-drunk on that "big" paycheck and run through the cash like water. We don't even consider how we are going to pay for our living expenses in the upcoming months. Sound familiar?

That's why we should always work with a Healthy Reserve account. The reason we need a three-month buffer is that we know that, as a consultant, artist, or entrepreneur, we're a lot more expendable than the average full-time employee. Indeed, we may have no idea when that next project or painting is going to sell or the next client is going to buy our services. Less job stability means less money stability. Less money stability increases the need for a money reserve to protect us from the ups and downs of variable paychecks. So, always, always build a Healthy Reserve account, and always live within your means.

Here's how to do that. If you're fairly sophisticated and already have a business checking account, fine. Then get yourself a business *savings* account, and use it as your Healthy Reserve. Have your banker connect the two electronically, and dump all of your consulting, entrepreneurial, or artist income into the *savings account*, or what we're now calling your Reserve.

Pay yourself on the first of each month by transferring *exactly* what you will need to cover your monthly Debt-Free Spending Plan—your personal living expenses—into your *personal* checking account. Then put exactly what you need to cover your business expenses into your business checking account. Have a Debt-Free Spending Plan for your business account, too. Your personal-necessities money goes into the personal checking account, while business payments go into the business checking account. Think of it this way: It's just as if you were getting a paycheck for both business and personal expenses, only in this model you're paying yourself in two allotments from your Reserve. The balance of your income stays in your Healthy Reserve Account to cover the months you get no paycheck.

If you don't have a business checking account (e.g., if you're a sole proprietor and don't generate enough in bank transactions to warrant a separate business account), then simply use your Healthy Reserve account (savings) to accomplish the same thing. Dump all of your paychecks into your Reserve, and pay yourself by depositing just what you need for the upcoming month into your personal checking account. Leave all overages in your reserve.

Why is this so critical? Because when we payday debt and run up credit lines, we put immense pressure on our budding new projects to succeed, and our desperation often contributes to their failure. So, fund everything you do, all the time, with solvency, and your creative and entrepreneurial projects will have the dignity of their own growth arc. Think *slow, steady steps*. Keeping a Healthy Reserve account and living within your means is the only way to do that.

Debit Cards versus Cash

What's always astounding to me, when I'm working with debtors, is how few of us have ever used our debit cards. Debit cards (of course, we really know this) work just as conveniently as credit cards, only the money comes straight out of our checking accounts. In other words, the age-old excuse that credit cards are just more *convenient* has been remedied for us. A debit card is just as convenient—so why aren't we using this miraculous tool?

We debtors are also particularly fond of taking large (or lots of small) amounts out at the ATM machine and having no idea how these amounts relate to what we're spending in each expense category. We treat the ATM as if it were a money *printing* machine—we take $100 or $200 out, spend it with no accountability, and then wonder why we don't know where our cash goes. And our debit card is sitting in our wallets the whole time, just as good as cash.

Do yourself a favor and utilize your debit card. Pay for everything you can with your debit card, and use minimal cash. Write down everything you spend in your Magic Little Notebook, which ensures you'll be staying within your Debt-Free Spending Plan. Any place that you've used your credit card will also accept your debit card—and the good news is, you'll have a receipt and a record of what you spent.

Using your debit card to stay accountable keeps you consistently drawing your Daily Needs expenses out of the same pool of money. That's important if you tend to get overwhelmed by your monthly finances. Fewer categories to account for—and less loose cash to get overwhelmed by—means less confusion.

For simple things like parking-meter money, bridge tolls, laundry quarters, and so on—things debit cards won't work for—just fund them in cash at the beginning of the month, and don't bother keeping track of them for each individual use. Your Debt-Free Spending Plan will reflect $10 in parking/toll money and $20 in laundry quarters (or whatever your personal totals are), each and every month. Stash the parking or toll quarters or dollars in your car and dump the laundry quarters in a jar. You'll have money for those items every month and you won't bother yourself about writing down anything more than the monthly totals you have allocated.

THE ENVELOPE METHOD VERSUS DEBIT CARDS

If it works better for you to use cash for your Daily Needs, then go to the bank and get the exact amounts for each expense category and put the cash in labeled envelopes. Don't even try to take the whole amount in 100s or 20s and assume you'll figure it out later. You'll never, ever do it—and you know it. Have *exact cash* for each Daily Needs envelope. Go to the bank with your envelopes in hand, already labeled—for example, "Food," "Fuel." "Drug Store Items." The theory is simple: You keep all of your Daily Needs money for the month in the labeled envelopes, and that's all you have to spend. When it's gone, it's gone. No more spending.

If you like this method, then fine—use it. But put your envelopes someplace safe, and take them out only when it's time to shop for that category item. (If you have addicted, troubled, or recovering kids, spouses, or partners in the house do not even *think* about using the cash-in-envelope method. Don't even set yourself up for that drama.)

Personally, I'm not a huge fan of the cash-in-envelope method; it requires me to have my envelopes with me whenever I need something for daily life. More often than not, I'm more likely to have my debit card with me. When I use my debit card, there's no change to mess around with, no cash versus debit balances to calculate, and no chance I'll "forget" I took money from one expense category or another.

One caution: If your debit card is also attached to a credit line, cut off the credit line. Right now—just make the call to the bank and cut it off. You've agreed to stop debting one day at a time, so don't even pretend to fool yourself about using your debit card while still running up more credit card debt. You'll shoot yourself in the foot, and none of the work you've done so far will matter.

Cutting off all your credit cards, credit lines, and borrowing is your charge here, but cutting off credit lines from your debit card is *essential* to your success with the Debt-Free Spending Plan. Live on what you earn. Put your monthly expense money into your checking account, use your debit card, and live within your means. No buts. No whining. Just show up and do it.

The Debt-Free Spending Plan is a simple tool that will lead you to a debt-free life faster than anything else I know of. It doesn't matter what your spending history is, how you were raised, or what money attitudes you grew up with. It doesn't require you to account for all the years of reckless spending or past debting. All it asks is that you start now—*today*—and use the tools given in this chapter to get free of your debting behavior and live within your means.

THE NINE STEPS TO A DEBT-FREE LIFE

1. Create a Debt-Free Spending Plan every month, before the month begins, based on the cash income you will receive.

2. Create a Bill-Paying Plan, based on the dates your cash is coming in.

3. Pay your bills on time, based on your Bill-Paying Plan.

4. Write your Daily Needs amounts in your Magic Little Notebook, by category, one on each page.

5. Use your debit card and your Magic Little Notebook to stay solvent, always checking your notebook before you buy anything to make sure you have enough money.

6. Use your Magic Little Notebook to stay solvent between categories—so if you overspend in one category, you take that amount out of another category.

7. Use cash only for small purchases like meter money, laundry money, and bridge tolls, funding a set amount for these needs each month.

8. Keep a tracking record of everything you spend, using the same simple categories as in your Debt-Free Spending Plan.

9. Allocate money for Savings, Vacation, and Fun—each month, no matter how small the amount.

Putting It All Together

The example below is what you will create each month, no matter what. Your Spending Plan consists of a summary statement of all of your income, how you're allocating it, your Bill-Paying Plan, and your tracking record. It's all in one place, saved and labeled by month for easy reference. And your Magic Little Notebook and debit card keep you living debt-free every day, every time you make a purchase.

Note once again that you can do the Debt-Free Spending Plan on paper, in a Word document, in Excel, or in a financial software program. You can use any app or program that uses all of the tools taught in this book. It doesn't matter which tools you use as long as you understand the structure of the Spending Plan and don't skip any steps. Here's our example, in all of its parts:

J'S DEBT-FREE SPENDING PLAN / JULY 2010

Monthly Spending Plan

Income

July 6 paycheck	$1,592.00
July 20 paycheck	1,592.00
Total	$3,184.00

Necessities

Bills	$2,094.00
Daily Needs	914.00
Total	$3,008.00

Balance

$3,184.00 (income)	
−3,008.00 (necessities)	
$176.00 (left over)	

Savings, Vacation, and Fun	+176.00
Fun (spend on anything I like)	50.00
Savings Account	80.00
Vacation Account	46.00
Total	176.00

Monthly Plan Detail

Bills	Due Date	Amount
Rent	1st	1,110.00
Car Payment	28th	394.00
Cell Phone	21st	80.00
Phone/Internet	7th	90.00
Health Insurance	10th	45.00 (my contribution)
Car Insurance	10th	91.50
Cable	N/A	N/A
Utilities	25th	25.00
Gym	7th	27.00
Newspaper Subscription	N/A	N/A
Movie Subscription	21st	8.00
Monthly Dues	N/A	N/A

Automatic Savings	10th	25.00
Credit card 1	27th	45.00 min
Credit card 2	25th	67.00 min
Bank Loan	28th	86.50 min
Parent/Friend Loan Repayment		[Not paying yet]
Total		2,094.00

Daily Needs	**Amount**
Food (Groceries)	250.00
Fuel	225.00
Parking/Tolls/Public Transit	10.00
Medical Co-Pays	30.00
Drug Store	25.00
Beauty/Personal Care	25.00
Dry Cleaning	30.00
Laundry Home (coin-ops for apartments)	20.00
Household	25.00
Postage	9.00
Clothing	40.00
Haircut	40.00
Office Supplies	10.00
Entertainment	20.00
Yoga	100.00
Child's Allowance	20.00
Cash Contributions	35.00
Total	914.00

Tracking Record

Food	**250.00**
7/8 Trader Joe's	35.19
7/9 Dean's Produce	23.19
7/15 Marina Market	29.17
7/16 Molly Stone's	7.50
7/17 Trader Joe's	25.33
Etc.	
Fuel	**225.00**
7/7 Union 76	44.19

7/16 Eagle Gas	45.12
Etc.	
Parking/Tolls/Public Transit	**10.00**
7/16 Bridge toll	4.00
Etc.	
Medical Co-Pays	**30.00**
7/10 Dr. Hughes	15.00
Etc.	

List each Daily Needs category

Bill-Paying Plan

July 6 Check	**Due Date**	**1,592.00**
Daily Needs		914.00
Fun, Savings, Vacation		176.00
Cell Phone	21st	80.00
Phone/Internet	7th	90.00
Health Insurance	10th	45.00 (my contribution)
Car Insurance	10th	91.50
Utilities	25th	25.00
Gym	7th	27.00
Automatic Savings	10th	25.00
Credit card 1	27th	45.00 min
Credit card 2	25th	67.00 min
Total		1,585.50
		Leaves +6.50 in checking

July 20 Check	**Due Date**	**1,592.00 + 16.50** **= \$1,598.50**
Rent for August	1st Aug	1,110.00
Car Payment	28th	394.00
Bank Loan	28th	86.50 min
Movie Subscription	21st	8.00
Total		1,598.50
		Exactly even

Magic Little Notebook
For Daily Needs. In a 3 × 5-inch notebook.

On one page:

Food	**250.00**
7/8 Trader Joe's	−35.19
	+214.81
7/9 Dean's Produce	−23.19
	+191.62
7/15 Marina Market	−29.17
	+162.45

Etc.

On another page:

Fuel	**225.00**
7/6 Eagle Gas Station	−27.35
	+197.65
7/14 Chevron Gas Station	−33.12
	+164.53

Etc.

On another page:

Dry Cleaning	**30.00**
7/10 A-1 Cleaners	−35.00
	−5.00
7/10 From Household	+5.00
	0

On another page:

Household	**20.00**
7/3 Walgreens - kitchen supplies	−7.23
	+12.77
7/10 To Dry Cleaning	−5.00
	+7.77

Etc.

That's it. That's the Debt-Free Spending Plan at a glance. It's simple. It's a summary of how much you have, how much you can spend, what you spent, when to pay your bills, and a Magic Notebook to keep you solvent with each purchase.

Will it take some time? Yes. Will you have to get used to writing things down? You bet. Will it feel tedious at first? Absolutely. Will you want to rebel, swear, lash out, or run dramatic scenarios of destruction in your head? You probably will. We all feel that stuff when we first begin. So what. Begin anyway. By the first month you'll be living debt-free, and by the third month all of this will feel like second nature. Is it detailed? Yes, it is. But it's not complicated. The whole Debt-Free Spending Plan is based on simple addition and subtraction—simple lists—and any one of us can handle that level of complexity.

Begin Today

Begin right now. If you haven't already crafted the pieces of your Debt-Free Spending Plan as you've been reading this book, do it now. Don't wait one more day. Your freedom is just a couple of hours away.

The Debt-Free Spending Plan is meant to be work, but simple work. You can do it. If you follow the Spending Plan and use its tools, you will always, always live debt-free and stress-free. Think of what a relief that will be. It's right here and it's within your grasp.

In the upcoming chapters we'll address short-term and long-term savings—and specifically, *our dream building*. We'll see how to free up extra cash and review Debt-Free Spending Plans for a couple. We'll address debt repayment and take a look at some real-world Debt-Free Spending Plans. We'll look at everything that will help us make money choices that enrich our lives and give us a sense of financial ease.

For now, though, do your Spending Plan. Pick up your keyboard or your pencil and do it now. No excuses. Your financial peace of mind is waiting for you, right here in *The Debt-Free Spending Plan*.

4

. . . . .

Deprivation Will Never Get You Debt-Free

A Plan for Everything We Need, Want, and Dream of

FOR THOSE OF us who have been in debt forever, the concept of saving may seem unnecessary or even wholly out of reach. *I've lived without savings my whole life and somehow I've made it—why should I bother now?* Here's why: *Because your savings are now going to take the place of your credit cards.* When you no longer use credit cards for anything, you no longer stress about money. So now you've got to have a stash of cash to cover you when the normal, yet unexpected "financial stuff of life" shows up at your front door.

Your savings are going to take the form of three personal priorities that are meaningful to your life. These priorities are: (1) a Healthy

Reserve, (2) a Short-Term Savings account, and (3) Fun Money and Special Project accounts. We'll talk about each of these in detail.

Why Have a "Healthy Reserve" Account?

When I first heard of the concept of a living-expense reserve account, I thought it was a little insane. Three months of living expenses sitting in a savings account? *In what kind of dream world would that be possible? And why would I want to tie up my cash like that even if I had it?*

Then I heard a friend of mine tell a story. He was working for a sports television network as a sales director, and he had increased their advertising income by more than 30 percent. When his salary review came up, the network director told him that, though he had terrific success—20 percent more than the goals set in his contract—they weren't going to be able to increase his salary or offer a bonus because the network's budget had suffered in other departments and they were down overall. And here's what having three months of living expenses socked away did for him: It gave him the power to negotiate a raise anyway and the power to walk away if they didn't reward his accomplishments. He didn't even argue. He simply said, "You're giving me a 25 percent salary increase, a bonus of $20,000, and a new car lease." They did.

It was the same for me, in reverse. I was in a fund-raising job in which I had delivered a 51 percent increase, but I was denied a promised raise because the organization's leaders were debting—running deficits 40 percent over budget. But I couldn't leave or even challenge them because I had no reserve and not enough savings. So, I had to stay until I found another job. All I could do was lobby them, get rejected, and get angrier until I had the cash to leave. Get it?

A Healthy Reserve offers us *options*. If we're in a bad relationship (personal or professional), a Healthy Reserve offers us the dignity of removing ourselves when we need to. Our reserve also offers us time. If our company goes belly-up and we're suddenly on the street looking for work for the first time in ten years, we've got *time*. If a recession hits and we lose our job, we've got a buffer—a period of time to weather the transition. When we have three months of living expenses socked away, a recession cannot rock us the way it does when we're living paycheck to paycheck.

Thus, a Healthy Reserve is just that—a savings account that you use in case of emergency. It's not for Christmas money, or new tires, or a last-minute trip, or because you splurged at Target. It's for job loss, transition times, a medical leave of absence—real, genuine emergencies.

So, here's how you begin. You open a savings account, and you put a small amount into this account every month. Make it an automatic deduction, if you can. Your long-term goal is to have enough money to cover three months of living expenses socked away in your Healthy Reserve and—this is important—*to not touch it unless there's a financial emergency.*

Your Healthy Reserve account is holy. It's your ticket to your first financial ease—freedom, choices, and feeling good about being able to take care of yourself in the event of a change or crisis. So, just begin. Don't worry about how much or how little you'll deposit. Just put a little bit away each month while you're learning to live within your means. If it's only $35 a month, then so be it. Even if it's $5, just start. And then give yourself a big cheer of congratulations. You've begun your Healthy Reserve.

You Also Need Short-Term Savings

So, what do you do for short-term needs, like new tires, dental expenses, or Christmas presents? You're not going to use your Healthy Reserve, because that's for emergencies. Instead, you'll create a Short-Term Savings account for everything not covered in your Debt-Free Spending Plan. As I mentioned before, you'll want to get as many of your bills on a monthly payment plan (car insurance, homeowner's insurance, property taxes, etc.) as possible. The fewer quarterly bills you have, the less money you'll have to save for them, and the more money you get to keep each month for your wants.

If you have special savings needs for particular wants—like travel, dinners out, saving for a house, a birthday, a clothing buy, a new computer—then you might want to have separate, special savings accounts for those items. (See box, below.) But even if you do that, you'll still need a general, all-purpose Short-Term Savings account. How come? Because unexpected things will always come up during the year that you'll need to pay for.

Like what? Your crown snapped in two and you've got to come up with $390 to cover your co-pay—or $950 to cover the whole thing. Your car tune-up—which you saved for—revealed a bad carburetor and it's going to cost another $400. You weren't realistic about your kids' camp costs and you need to fund another $300. Your Short-Term Savings account covers these unexpected, unforeseen expenses without your ever having to use a credit card.

At first, your Short-Term Savings and Healthy Reserve accounts may have only a few dollars deposited in them each month. Don't worry about that now. Just begin. Mine started out with $25 in each account—a far cry from the three months of living expenses or enough to cover a new dental crown. In a very short time, though—two years, actually—I saved enough for a fully stocked Healthy Reserve and had a viable Short-Term Savings account as well. There's a consciousness to all of this financial stuff, and when you start to live within your means and save for what's meaningful for you, you somehow accrue more than you think you will.

So, even if it's only a few dollars a month, fund your Short-Term Savings account every month.

MULTIPLE SAVINGS ACCOUNTS

One of the joys of having multiple pools of cash stashed away is that when you have a financial need, there are multiple places to look for the money. When my husband took his car to the mechanic recently for an oil change and tune-up, the bill ended up being $699 more than the original quote. Since he had money in his Car Repairs Savings account, his Short-Term Savings account, and a little money left over from last month's living expenses, he was able to cover the whole thing in cash. Even though there was an extra, unexpected charge, he didn't go into debt. That's what "meaningful savings" is all about.

In our house, we each have multiple savings accounts—several of which are designated for things we love to do, want to buy, or want to experience. And, we each also have a Short-Term Savings account and a Healthy Reserve. Then, every month we put money into accounts for our wants: a "dining out" account, a "travel" account, a "new computer" account, a "CD Recording Fund" account, and so on.

How come so many accounts? Because we're debtors, and if we leave all of our savings in one account, we're sure to spend it on something other than what we really want—meaning we'll deprive ourselves again. When we deprive ourselves, our propensity for debting just grows. So we fund, in cash savings, what's truly meaningful to us. Even if the big-ticket item we want—like three months in Italy—seems out of reach now, we fund it anyway in small amounts. "Money miracles" occur out of *intention*, and so we show up with an account that commits us to what we really, really want.

Fun Money and Special Projects Accounts

I promised we'd address that critical element that's been missing so long from our debt-pressured lives—that haunting three-letter word: f-u-n. The thing is, what we thought would make us happy or bring us more fun—spending whatever we wanted and using our credit lines to fund it—actually didn't bring us joy. The little bit of fun that our purchases may have brought us in the moment was weighted with knowing that we couldn't pay for them, and later we felt heavy with the burden of debt. As the debts piled up, the "fun" of debting turned manic-depressive—we were giddy with our purchases for a little while, but quickly afterward we were bummed out and stressed with our rising balances. So clearly, we need to redefine "fun."

THE RIGHT STUFF: DEBT-FREE FUN

Genuine fun brings joy, lightness, relaxation, freedom, exploration, delight, laughter, satisfied curiosity, and a light heart. Debt brings none of these. So anything we've labeled "fun" that has the weighty, pressure-cooker, ricochet-boomerang-backwash effect on the soul that debt brings does not count anymore. If we're going to get out of this mess of debt and its bad by-products, we've got to set ourselves straight on the terminology. We've got to be rigorously honest. Fun that later turns into excruciating soul pain is not really fun at all. It's an addictive hit—and it's bringing a whammy pain response in the morning.

Fun that is paid for in cash, experienced with no regrets, lives on in the soul as the delight of being alive, a joy in living. It brings a sharing of ourselves, during and after the fun, with an experience of ease, contentment, and happiness running through our veins. It's contagious, that joy, and it lifts everyone else in the room. That's real fun.

If we're honest with ourselves, most of us would admit that we've been carrying the twenty-ton weight of our debts around with us for most of our lives, and it hasn't—not by a long shot—felt fun. So, given that we're debtors, our fun has to be debt-free in order to qualify as bringing lightness and joy. You know it and I know it. So we need to rid ourselves of the thought process that living debt-free is cutting out some of our fun.

Living within your Debt-Free Spending Plan will—I promise— bring you some of the first genuine joy and delight you've had in years.

HOW TO FUND YOUR FUN

What do you love? What do you enjoy? What makes you happy? What have you always wanted to do? Take a moment and quickly write down ten things. Don't think too much—just write. Once you have your list, figure out which things on your list cost money. Have you always wanted to paint? What would canvases and paints cost? Have you wanted to learn how to fly a small airplane? What do lessons cost? Have you always wanted to go to Africa? What's the price tag on that trip? Don't leave it vague. Apply the "three contrasting quotes" rule (see below), get clarity, and make a note of the cost. Better yet, put the amount on the top of your Spending Plan as a financial goal.

By now, you may already have constructed your Debt-Free Spending Plan and are beginning to live with it. But you're going to need something to keep you motivated to live within your means, right? Here it is: Create a savings account to fund what you love. It's that simple. Take an item or two—or five—from your list and open multiple savings accounts for each thing you want to do or have. Fund the accounts every month with a small amount of cash—whatever works within your Debt-Free Spending Plan. When you live within your means, you get to fund what you love. When you don't, your life becomes all about bills and debt repayment—not a very light-hearted outlook, is it?

You may be thinking, *Why should I try so hard to save for things that I want? Shouldn't I just spend every dime getting myself out of debt?* No. How come? Because you're learning to live—and live well—on what you earn, on what you bring in. Living within your means and funding what you love to do bring you into the present moment. It generates contentment. It allows you to relax.

Every time we engage in vagueness with our money, overspending or debting at the grocery store, or blowing $200 at the bulk warehouse on mega-packs of socks or gallon jugs of olive oil, we steal from ourselves, from the things that would delight us. Fun, delight, joy, and the peace of mind that comes from funding the things we love with cash means we're better workers, friends, family members, and spouses. We're just easier to live with. We're living in the present moment, with no particular financial angst.

So begin now, and start savings for genuine, real-world, meaningful fun for yourself.

Weddings, Vacations, and Special-Event Debting

Weddings, anniversary parties, vacations, honeymoons, graduations, bar and bat-mitzvahs, quinceaneras, "coming-out" parties, and all other one-time, special events are sources of major debting for most of us, so let's get this and get it now: *You can only spend whatever you've saved in cash and not one damn dime more.*

Can you use your credit cards or borrow against your house if event expenses get out of hand? *Absolutely not.* The whole point of learning to live within your means is to help you to never—ever—enter the "out of hand" financial realm again.

There's nothing that gets us into huge amounts of debt faster than special-event debting. We feel an expectation to be extravagant because it's a one-time thing. And, since it's never going to happen again, we feel like we're *supposed* to make it "wonderful"—and most often that means overspending and going into debt.

Worse yet, we may be pressured by our families, especially if we're not the only ones footing the bill. Our parents may say: "We have thirty family friends that must get an invitation to this wedding or we'll insult them." Our children may guilt us: "But Sara got a sweet sixteen on a cruise ship—and I want one!" Our siblings may insist that we do "our part": "Listen, I don't care if you don't have the money. We're all pitching in equal amounts for Mom's eightieth, so put it on your credit card and shut up about it!"

By now, you should have cut up, canceled, or frozen all of your credit cards anyway. Even if you haven't, know this: Special-event debting is the fastest way to plague yourself with guilt and fear, decimating your finances and your happiness for a good, long time. So, make a pledge to yourself right now that you will not, ever, fund a special event with anything other than cash. Period.

SO, HOW DO I FUND A "BIG DAY"?

If you're not going to use your credit cards for your "big day" event, then what do you do? This is what you do: You save for it in a special savings account, and then you create—you guessed it!—a Debt-Free Spending Plan for it based on the cash you have.

Any special event can be subject to a Debt-Free Spending Plan. Got a wedding coming up? A trip to the Caribbean? A fiftieth wedding anniversary party for your folks? Great. Open a savings account specifically for your event and put an amount aside from your Spending Plan every month. Once you have saved as much as you reasonably can, make a Spending Plan for your event. *You don't get to spend one single cent until you have a Spending Plan, and not one dollar more than you have.*

That means you're going to have to downsize your sky's-the-limit expectations in order to live within your means. It means you're going to have to give up grandiosity and Event-of-a-Lifetime mentality. It means you have to be realistic, honest, and hard-core with yourself about what you have and what that can buy. The good news is you will learn how to use your creativity rather than your credit cards.

Instead of using your credit line or refinancing the house for $40,000 to pay for your daughter's bat mitzvah, you're going to have to be inventive and innovative. That's a skill you're going to use over and over again, throughout your lifetime. It's also the skill that's going to keep you sane around your money.

If your family pressures you to spend more than you have, you simply share your numbers. Even if it embarrasses you, you let the numbers help set your financial boundaries: "I'm sorry, Mom and Dad, but we have $3,000 tops for food in our Wedding Spending

Plan, and so sixty-five guests is the maximum we can invite. Our present to ourselves is to start our marriage debt-free." Trust me: It'll make you feel eighteen times freer to say "we can't afford that" rather than running up your credit line to appease your family.

And don't fall for the parental ploy, "We'll pay for the food for thirty more guests." *How come?* Because *all* of your other expenses will go up proportionally—chairs, tables, centerpieces—and you'll end up paying those costs and running up your totals. Set your boundaries with your family with your Spending Plan, and live by them.

THE "THREE CONTRASTING QUOTES" RULE

Here's a general rule of thumb for planning special events (or any major purchase): Always have clarity about what things cost, and *always get clear quotes before you commit*. My rule for myself is simple: I get three contrasting quotes for any major purchase. Caterers? Three quotes. Airline tickets? Three quotes. Wedding dress? Three quotes. (This goes for all major purchases, things like car and health insurance, vehicle purchases, rent or mortgage, and so on. What you're looking for is *clarity* on which price best fits your Spending Plan.)

My husband and I recently paid for an entire, beautiful wedding for eighty people for less than $10,000—including our wedding bands. Sound like too little? It wasn't. We had a Debt-Free Spending Plan. We shopped for caterers whom we could afford and found an upscale, fine-dining Italian restaurateur who did an amazing job for us. We rented the tables and set them up ourselves with white tablecloths in my mother-in-law's backyard. For our ceremony, we found a lovely grass-filled site with a small Greco-Roman temple facing the mountains that cost us less than $200, and we brought in a company to set up chairs for $300. We had tuxes and beautiful gowns and gorgeous flowers—but our expenses were proportional to our income. We stayed within our means. And, we saved another $8,000 for a three-week trip to Bali. We came home with extra cash and without any guilt.

Did we miss the $2,000 sushi hors d'oeuvres? No. We had delicious food and stayed stress-free. Did we miss the three-tiered Champagne waterfall? No. We had fabulous prosecco, generated no angst, and went on an incredible honeymoon.

Catching my drift? It doesn't matter what the event is. Make a Debt-Free Spending Plan for it and live within your means. No ifs, ands, or buts.

SPENDING PLANS FOR SPECIAL EVENTS AND VACATIONS

On vacations (especially out of the country, when you may be working with cash and no receipts), the Magic Little Notebook becomes even more important. First, you won't be using a tracking record (on computer or paper) most of the time, so your Magic Little Notebook becomes your Spending Plan and your tracking record in one. What my husband and I do is this: We create a Spending Plan for our vacation, give ourselves a daily average of cash to spend for expenses, and list what we spend in our Magic Little Notebook. It looks like this:

On one page:

June 26th	US$200.00 a day
Breakfast	10.00
Drinks	15.00
Snack	12.00
Water	3.00
Snorkeling	35.00
Dinner	60.00
Total	135.00

If we don't spend our $200 in one day, the extra rolls over to an "extra" page.

On the next page:
Extra:
7/26   +65.00

This way we always stay within our Vacation Spending Plan; we don't gouge our back-at-home expenses, and we do not debt. And, if we have overage cash and want to splurge on something mid-trip, we can use our "extra" money for it. (Miracle of all miracles, we've come home with extra cash on a number of trips! That's not something we ever would have experienced before without a Debt-Free Spending Plan.)

Now, take a look at a Wedding Spending Plan. First, we do the exact same thing we do with our monthly Spending Plan: We make a Plan, get a Magic Little Notebook, and use a tracking record. Our Spending Plan looks like this:

Wedding Spending Plan: $8,900

	Plan	Actual
Wedding Bands	1,250.00	1,210.00
Invitations (hand-made)		
Paper	20.00	22.50
Postage	40.00	33.60
Envelopes	24.00	21.00
	84.00	77.10
Flowers		
Sue from farmer's market		
$3/bunches of wildflowers × 12 tables	36.00	36.00
$15 × 3—wildflower bouquets—bridal	45.00	45.00
$12 × 3 men's flowers	36.00	36.00
$15 × 2 mothers	30.00	38.00
	147.00	155.00
Music		
Band for Reception Music	600.00	600.00
Ceremony music	200.00	200.00
Etc.		

Our Magic Little Notebook looks like this:

On one page:

Wedding Bands	1,250.00
3/4 Michelle Flynn Jeweler	−1,210.00
	+40.00

On another page:

Invitations	84.00
4/1 Paper	−22.50
	+61.50
5/3 Postage	−33.60
	+27.90
4/15 Envelopes	−21.00
	+6.90
6/12 to Flowers	−5.00
	+1.90

On another page:

Flowers	150.00
6/12 Sue from Farmer's Market	−155.00
	−5.00
6/12 from Invitations	+5.00
	0

If you go over in one category, it has to come out of another category. You always use our Magic Little Notebook, and you always stay solvent. If you spend only what you have, it will require a bit more of your ingenuity, but you will always stay sane around special events. If you have pressure-cooker relatives insisting you spend more than you can afford, you just share your Debt-Free Spending Plan dollar amounts and set a boundary. *You will only fund what you have cash for.* Even the most dogged insistence can be silenced with real numbers and a debt-free line drawn firmly in the sand.

Simple, But Not Always Easy

You may be thinking, *It can't be that simple.* I have news for you: It really is. When you live within your means, you can always put something aside for your wants. You've already planned for everything you need. You have a plan for your Bills, a plan for your Daily Needs, a Healthy Reserve, and some Short-Term Savings. And the rest—ta dah!—is for *you*. Over time, your relationship to saving money will change, and you'll have a Healthy Reserve that will cover *anything* out of the ordinary, including "emergencies." And you'll *still* have money for fun, entertainment, clothing and food, and car repairs—every month.

Once you've set up your Debt-Free Spending Plan and your Savings, Vacations, and Fun Money, you may find that you have a hard time getting yourself to spend the cash you've allotted. When I first started working my plan, I had been overspending for so long that I felt that, now that I had accountability, I should just hang on to as much of my cash as I could. That's a natural response. But here's the thing that finally bowled me over: If I spent my $50 in clothing money one month—guess what? There would be another $50 the next month, and another $50 the month after that. There would always be more money for the things I needed because I was going to plan for them every month! I could spend my $50 and know there would always be more—amazing!

Revelation: It was truly stunning to realize that I was *supposed* to have money every month for the things I needed to live. It was even more stunning to realize that when I allotted money for my needs, and spent within my means, I felt great about myself. I could take care of myself on my income, live decently, and live without debt. Even when my income was low and I was starting from scratch, living within my means brought more self-esteem than all the overspending ever had.

Learn to Live Well First

When my husband and I began living together, his debting weakness was going out to dinner, running up restaurant tabs on his credit cards. To make his Debt-Free Spending Plan work, it was important that he allocate a reasonable amount of cash each month for dining out so that he could experience funding his wants on the cash he had. Over time, after he knew that he could live contentedly on the money he was earning without debting, he was able to use his Spending Plan to address a larger portion of his debt repayment.

I believe it's important to choose the philosophy that will govern your Debt-Free Spending Plan. I'm not a fan of putting large amounts of your living expense cash into debt repayment, especially at first. If you've been debting to meet your needs, then you need to experience what it's like to live within your means—and live reasonably and proportionally well on that money *first*—before dealing with large-chunk debt repayment. (We'll talk about what reasonable debt repayment plans looks like in Chapter 6.)

So, begin to allocate Fun Money and a reasonable amount for Savings every month—they are both at the heart of any working Debt-Free Spending Plan.

5

. . . . .

To Cut or Not to Cut
Taking a Reasonable Look at
What You Can and Can't Afford

MOST OF US who are debtors will be overspending in several of our Daily Needs or Bills categories while depriving ourselves in others. We're in debt, but we're getting $200 haircuts and trying to scrape by on not enough food money. We're getting $115 facials, and then not saving for much-needed new tires. We're spending $800 a month eating meals out, and then debting to pay for our dry cleaning, our gym membership, or our kids' school clothes. And this is where we're going to have to *get real with ourselves* to make our Debt-Free Spending Plan work.

Our Daily Needs—and even our Bills, for that matter—need to be *proportional to the amount of money we bring home every month*. If we already know we can't afford that haircut, or we can't afford to eat out three times a day and we're doing it anyway, then we're sinking our ship further and further down into the mud. If we know we don't have the money to buy $250 worth of vitamins at our chiropractor's office (that we could certainly find online for much less), but we pony up anyway because we're embarrassed, can't speak up, or feel entitled, know that we're acting out of more than just emotion. *We're acting from a lack of clarity about what is a proportional expense in relation to our income.*

So, am I saying you should go without a decent haircut? Am I saying you can never eat out? Am I saying you shouldn't have vitamins? No. I'm saying that you and only you can stop your overspending. Yes, you do get to choose how you spend your money, but you're the adult here—and you have to take care of *all* of your needs. If $250 is more than your monthly food allotment, and there's no extra cash in your Spending Plan, then knock it off with the chiropractor's vitamins. If you've got only $800 a month for Daily Needs, after paying your Bills, then you're not going to be in the market for a $200 a month haircut or $400 for four rounds of golf.

I'm also not saying that you have to go without services and supplies—or even luxuries. What I am saying is that you'll have to employ a little *ingenuity* to get them. Why? Because you're going to stop charging all of those items and find cheaper ways to get your needs met—ways that allow you to live within your means and still get what you need. You're going to use your creativity, not your credit cards. More important, you're going to *balance* your expenses—meaning you're going to have reasonable amounts for each need, in proportion to your income, so that you don't deprive yourself or go into debt.

Cutting Means Financial Freedom

First off, we have to agree that it's worth it to make some cuts. Why are we bothering? Here's the point: When we make cuts to things we can live without for a while—essentially creating a downsized

Spending Plan for a short period of time—we can fund more of our immediate wants and needs *in cash*, more savings, and more of our long-term financial goals. And why is that important? Because by funding our wants, savings, and the long-term goals that are meaningful to us, we stay out of debt.

What you're going to learn to do is to stop overspending at the boutique, crazily priced grocery store so you can have a paid-for vacation. You'll stop the unaccountable overbuying at the Super-Size Warehouse to pay for that round of golf in cash. You'll live on reasonable amounts for your needs, and you'll save for a trekking trip to the Himalayas, a retirement party, or a new road bike. Get it? *Cutting is about becoming reasonable with your Bills and Daily Needs so that you can keep more of your cash for what you really, truly want.*

On your first pass at writing down your Daily Needs, you were probably over your income anyway, right? Most of us are. Cutting means we stop the train wreck of debt and start getting back on the rails of solvency. But being realistic and proportional in our spending goes a step further—it asks that we look at things we can live without, things we can downsize, so that our spending is in line with our values. What do we love? *That's* where our extra cash should be going.

Cutting also offers something that most of us debtors have never had: savings. We talked about Savings accounts in the previous chapter: why they are important, why it's good to create specific accounts, why it's important to make your savings accounts meaningful to you. But there's another reason. Cash savings mean you have money choices and life choices. Funding your wants and funding your savings offers you the choice to make the moves in your life that will protect you, support you, enliven you, and relieve you from situations that are not good for you. That's financial freedom. And you don't need a million dollars to get it. You can have that freedom on the income you have right now.

Cutting expenses also offers a magical, ingenious strategy: The ability to live on less if you have a special project you'd like to accomplish.

Do you have a film you want to edit? A book you want to write? A clothing line you want to start? When you cut expenses and build a Healthy Reserve, you can pass on the full-time day job for a while, live on less, and get your dreams kick-started.

In the remainder of this chapter, we'll first discuss how you can reduce expenses in your Daily Needs categories and then focus on how you can do the same in your monthly Bills spending.

Making Cuts in Your Daily Needs Categories

Cutting Daily Needs is relatively simple in theory. All we need to do is allot less money in each category of spending to free up some more cash, right? In practice, though, it's a bit more challenging. How come? Because this is the arena in which we've been vaguely, mindlessly, consistently overspending. This is the arena in which we have had no clarity, in which we exercise and act out our feelings of entitlement, rebellion, depression spending, "shopping therapy," or keeping-up-with-the-Joneses. We go shopping—regularly—with no idea how much we really need, how much we can really afford, or how much we should be spending on each expense item.

What happens inside us when we debtors go to the shi-shi grocery store in the hipster neighborhood and fill four containers at the olive bar at $20 per pound? What's going on in our minds when we go to the tip-me-over-with-the-prices meat counter and feel somehow like we *should* be able to pay $27 a pound for lamb? What's at work in us when we know we can't afford to buy the latest i-something gadget, or pay the higher monthly usage costs to run the thing, and we try to convince ourselves that we need it?

This is what's happening: We're feeling *entitled*, and when we feel entitled, we're apt to use our credit cards. When we use credit for entitlement purchases, it's more than rebellion. It's because we have a lack of clarity *in real and proportional numbers* about what we can and cannot fund with our salary and income. All of that is about to change.

Your Daily Needs is the spending area in which you first begin to get solvent. If the very thought of cutting these items makes you panic, you're not alone. If you feel belligerent about it ("Who do you think you are to tell me I can't shop at Whole Foods?"), rebellious ("I don't have to do a damn thing I don't want to do—it's my money!"), or panicked ("I don't know how the hell I'm ever going to live on what I actually make. . . "), do not despair. All of us—every one of us—who have been in trouble with debt have experienced all of that balking and panic when we first sat down to cut. It's normal human emotion. Let it bubble up and pass like clouds in the sky. Then, ready yourself to take the next indicated step—that is, to *cut* some things.

One more thing: Just because you're about to cut some spending items, that doesn't mean you get to go blank. This is not rocket science. So, don't indulge in the money glaze-over. You know what I'm talking about: You suddenly go so vague on yourself that you forget how to add. Stay in. This is the place where you start to get free— the real-life juncture at which you actually figure out how to pay for all of your needs in cash. Think how amazing that's going to feel! Think what a self-esteem booster it's going to be at the end of the month to have not one damn dime of debt added to your balances!

Following is a list of spending areas where you can cut. Once again, I'm not telling you which ones you should or should not cut. That's your job. Figure out which of these overspending areas match your experience and your need for more clarity and cash, and make cuts in those categories. (A general rule of thumb: If you have intense resistance to cutting a particular overspending area, that's probably a good sign that you need to cut there.) When we start the Debt-Free Spending Plan, most of us can stand to cut in many, if not all, of these areas. Take what works and leave the rest, but remember: You have to make *all* of your categories work, *in cash*, proportionally covering all of your needs.

GROCERIES

Find low-priced, neighborhood, ethnic, and discount food stores and buy once a week. Stop it, stop it, stop it with the high-end, "whole paycheck" grocery stores. I don't care how organic they are, how cute they seem, how hip and urbane and boutique they are—you can't afford them right now.

This spending area is always a stickler with my clients. They feel a hip, urban need to buy in chic spots, or an entitled suburban need to purchase where it's lavish and upscale. Let me make this clear for you: *The more you vaguely spend in overpriced grocery stores, the more debt stress you will have in your life.* If you're in debt at all and you're shopping in these stores, you are gouging your ability to pay for your life's needs in cash. Food will be your biggest expense per month after your Bills, and to buy with a lack of clarity and lack of real value is to sabotage your entire monthly financial picture. You are bringing debt and stress to yourself, your partner relationship, and your family.

There are certainly other Daily Needs categories where debting and vague overspending are an issue, but this particular category is one of the best places to put on the brakes, and to do it now. It's insane to spend money on mindless, high-ticket food items (that essentially come from the same warehouses) that are marketed for "cute" value, when you can't pay for your dental work or take a vacation without a credit card. You are *stealing* money from yourself and your solvency here, so please, please stop doing it. The ethnic or discount markets won't be swanky, but they will save you as much as 50 percent on your groceries and will still offer you plenty of good, fresh food all month long.

ORGANIC PRODUCE AND MEAT

Buy what's lowest in pesticides and purchase organic only for a few fruits, vegetables, or special occasion meats. We debtors and overspenders love to argue about the need to keep debting in order to buy "organic." And let me be clear again: *You do not get to debt or gouge your income in order to buy organic.* If it's a priority for you, then go online and get the list of "the ten dirtiest and cleanest fruits and vegetables" (re: pesticides), and buy the clean ones. Or get a "Farm Fresh to You" service that drops off a box of organic fruits and vegetables at your door for a set price—you can get one for as little as $35 a week—and make the box last all week long. (You don't even have to shop for it!)

Better yet, join a community garden if organic is vital to you, and grow your own vegetables. If meat is an issue, then shop online for an organic cattle raiser (like Beltaneranch.com); buy one-quarter or one-eighth of an animal, and put it in your freezer for the year. (Save for it first, by putting a little aside each month, and buy yearly.) But no matter what option you choose, you do not get to debt or gouge your Spending Plan in order to buy swanky-looking produce, meat, or market products.

BULK PRODUCTS STORES

Avoid bulk stores at all costs. Buy only what you need weekly from regular grocers and do not ever "stock up." "Stocking up" is code for overspending. We debtors like to buy, and we like to buy mindlessly—and then throw up our hands and say, "My finances are just such a mess and I can never figure out how they get that way!" They got that way by spending without clarity, and the fastest way to spend without clarity is to buy in bulk warehouse stores. Unless you are feeding a family of eight, there is absolutely no reason to shop bulk. Can your family really eat enough pork ribs for twenty people? Are you really going to eat pork ribs all month long until they're all gone? Not likely. So stop doing that.

Buy what you need, week by week, in affordable stores and *do not even attempt to stock up.* Get used to the notion of having enough to live, every week—amounts that, I guarantee you, will be less than you think you need—without hoarding. Debtors are often consumed with the fear of "not enough," so know that you will have to train yourself to buy only for the week at hand. If you've saved the cash for a big party, then by all means use the bulk warehouse store to buy what you need. Otherwise, stay away.

We need to cure ourselves of the notion that we can stockpile groceries and still have enough food money (or gas money, etc.) to live all month long. The bulk warehouse will ruin the resolve of even the most repentant debtor. First, it will tempt you to buy size quantities that appear to be "deals," but that actually result in a half gallon of mayonnaise or ketchup or olives that no human family can reasonably consume before they grow into biological mold experiments. Waste is a huge factor. Second, bulk stores entice us to buy things we don't need ("These socks and T-shirt packs are such an amazing deal—I'll get three packs!"), stuff we may already have at home and truly have no need for. So unless you have a major purchase or a party, don't buy bulk and don't even go to the store.

PREPARED FOOD

Buy affordable food and cook it at home. This is a sticky point with singles or for spouses who are on their own for meals. And you already know what I'm going to say: You can't afford to buy prepared food right now. This is the same issue as the swanky grocery and the organic stand— you are going to have a limited amount of money for food each week, and that's it. So, if you go to the prepared counter for last-minute meals, you're going to be out of cash long before your week is through.

Remember what we did with the creation of our Debt-Free Spending Plan? We took the total amount of our food allotment for the month—let's say $400—and divided it by the number of Saturdays (grocery shop day). Let's say there are five Saturdays in the month. Then you've got $80 *total* for groceries each week. Two meals of $40 worth of prepared food is going to gouge you in the basics area—you're still going to need milk, fruit, vegetables, bread, meat, fish, lunch meat—all that. So stop with the prepared counters.

You're building an entertainment category into your Spending Plan, and if you can afford it, a dining-out category as well. So skip the pricey prepared stuff, and use your dining/entertainment money for a really nice restaurant meal to reward yourself for your debt-free efforts. If you're not gouging in other areas (meaning you're stashing enough cash in your savings), then go ahead and build in a take-out category into your Spending Plan. But no gouging.

LUNCHES

Take your lunch to work at least three days a week. Work lunches are a big drain on monthly Spending Plans. When my husband and I were working on his Debt-Free Spending Plan, we realized he was spending almost $200 a month on lunches and another $150 on coffee drinks—and he had no travel account. Since travel was a bigger priority for him, he decided to do a three-fifths approach: He would buy lunch meat for sandwiches (or burritos, or whatever) at an affordable store like Trader Joe's, eat at work, and two days a week he would take himself to his favorite Mexican lunch spot. That meant he did not have to completely lose the pleasure of lunching out, but it gave him cash to travel (a coastal inn, a weekend away) very regularly. In the first year of his Spending Plan, we went away on his travel money five times. Once he started experiencing the freedom of traveling on cash, eating lunch at work became a small price to pay.

If you can't really afford to eat lunch out at all—that is, if your Spending Plan is so close to the bone that you have very little cash for entertainment or fun—then cut buying lunches out altogether. It will not kill you to bring your lunch to work. (It may also help you to cut down on extra calories at your noonday meal.) Make your lunch the night before and be done with it. Then, at the end of the month, if you have any extra money in your Spending Plan, you can treat yourself and buy a lunch out.

COFFEE

Get a coffee maker and brew your own at home. What did we do before the advent of the chic coffee-bar drink? We made coffee at home, that's what—and we were more solvent. I know it's a great pleasure to go to a Peet's, a Starbucks, or a Coffee & Tea Leaf and get a frou-frou coffee drink. But here's the thing: We've been "treating" our-selves to all kinds of things we can't afford and can't pay for, and then we're up in the middle of the night, sweating over our debting issues. We're sick to our stomachs when we try to pay our bills. Yet we still feel entitled, and we don't think we should ever have to be reined in. Our attitude and our overspending are causing us so much grief or low-level anxiety that we can't take it anymore.

So I'm going to sum this up for you in one simple sentence: *If you are debting to live, then you cannot afford to buy coffee drinks on a regular basis.* Period. Coffee drinks purchased several days a week (not even daily, which a lot of us do) will represent more than $150 a month—sometimes up to $250. If you have no savings, no vacation fund, and are paying for your kids' camp costs with credit cards, then you have no business setting foot in the coffee house. Get it?

Do you want to use your Fun Money for a frappachino? Then go ahead. Do you have extra food money at month's end? Then spend it on coffee drinks, if you like. Does your Spending Plan allow you to set aside a specific amount each month to cover the coffee bar? Then build it in. But if your income is being stretched to cover your basic needs (like food and fuel), and you have no savings, you are not going to be in the market for $150 worth of coffee drinks each month. Buy yourself some gourmet beans, grind them up, and get a coffee maker for $12 at a discount store. If and when your Spending Plan can han-dle it, allot an amount each month for coffee—say $25 or $50, and live within that amount all month long.

A COFFEE TRADE-OFF

My husband solved "the coffee issue" simply by drinking a reg-ular cup of coffee (rather than a cappuccino) at his favorite cof-fee bar, and allotting $40 for it every month. If you can make it work in your Spending Plan, then treat the coffees like lunches out: Make coffee at home three days a week, and buy it out the other two. Or just treat yourself to a coffee drink on weekends. No matter what you choose, this item *must* be proportional to your other expenses each month. Meaning, you can't gouge for coffee.

FUEL

Buy what's cheapest, and buy it weekly. Obviously, even the most diligent Debt-Free Spending Plan adherence cannot control the whims of the oil companies. That said, even if gasoline prices do fluctuate, you will be able to field the change simply by adjusting your Spending Plan up a bit in the fuel category. That means those dollars have to come from someplace else, meaning you'll have to adjust another category down. But that's not nearly as panicky at it sounds. Once you have clarity about what you're spending, if expenses go up in one category—like fuel—you simple massage your Spending Plan a bit and make the adjustment. It somehow always works out.

That said, once you have the monthly total you're working with for fuel, you can help yourself by buying weekly. Once again, buying weekly will help keep you solvent. *How come?* Because weekly buying makes you aware of what you're spending every seven days, and helps you mentally *plan* for weeks in which you have greater fuel needs. Going to visit your dad and it's a two-hour drive? Have a class this month that's going to have you driving more than an hour each way? Are you the carpool mom this week? Then you may have to adjust your Spending Plan up a bit for that week—meaning you have to adjust from alternate weeks or take that cash from another category. If you need more than one tank of gas per week, then calculate your Spending Plan to cover what you'll need. The point is, we buy as needed, based on our monthly allotments, and we *do not stock up.*

I do the same thing for fuel as I do for groceries: Once I have my monthly total, I divide the monthly amount by the number of Saturdays (or whatever my shopping day is) and I purchase only that amount.

If you don't drive, but you use Zipcars, rentals, or forms of public transportation, then build a category into your Spending Plan that covers those costs. If you use rentals at irregular but frequent intervals, then create a Savings account that covers you when you need a car.

DRY CLEANING

Find an affordable dry cleaner and limit the amount of clothes you dry clean. Dry cleaning is another easy place to vaguely gouge your monthly Spending Plan. You're busy, you want some downtime (for God's sake), and so you mindlessly drop off everything you can at the dry cleaners—resulting in a $100+ bill when you pick up your clothes. Or, you save up all of your dry cleaning for four months and rack up a whopping $300 in charges, gouging your money for living expenses. Don't do that anymore.

If you can afford regular dry cleaning, then fine. But if not, and if you know you have to wear suits to work and you need clean, pressed shirts every day, then plan for it. Wash, dry, and iron at least *some* of your washable items and plan for your weekly dry cleaning. If you have five shirts to clean and need them five days of the week, at $5 per shirt, that's more than $100 a month. If your Spending Plan doesn't support that kind of expenditure proportional to other items, then—you guessed it—you're going to have to wash and dry more of your clothes. When I was broke and first working my Debt-Free Spending Plan, I didn't wear a lot of the things in my wardrobe that needed dry cleaning because I couldn't afford the monthly expense. Remember, we're going to go to whatever lengths we must to end the stress of debt in our lives. The soul ease of no debt will pay off much, much more in peace of mind than a dry-cleaned shirt.

DRUG STORE ITEMS

Shop in discount stores and buy only what you need. Drug store expenditures have been a popular mindless spending category for many of us. We go to the super discount store and try to stock up on everything from contact solution to toilet paper. Stop doing that. Once again, *we don't stock up.* We buy what we need and only what we need. In the drug store category, I go to the discount store once a month, buy my contact solutions, lotions, creams, and that's it for the month. I don't spend one dime more unless I still have some money in my Spending Plan for the expense.

It should be obvious by this point that your Debt-Free Spending Plan will change the way you shop. You will not "run out" and buy this or that. You'll always have a *plan.* Note that drug store items are different from food and fuel, in that you can reasonably buy your supplies once a month if necessary. So you plan according to your own needs. Do you have to drive for affordable drug store items? Then maybe you'd rather buy them monthly rather than weekly so you only have to drive once. Or you may want to buy as needs arise and buy locally. If so, you'll keep deducting all month long from your drug store category total until it's gone. Get the idea? Make it work for you, depending on your specific needs.

BEAUTY ITEMS

Shop drug stores and discount stores, and pass on all pricey products. Most women and some men I know overspend considerably on beauty products. There is such a marketing racket in specialized skin and haircare products in our culture that we have come to believe we can't get by without a $98 a month, mail-order skincare line or a department store counter "anti-aging" gel that costs $139 an ounce. So, we're going to have to go back to the proportional argument: If you have only $50 for entertainment and very little for a vacation fund each month—and you're spending $90 or $120 or $150 a month on makeup and skin products, then you're going to need to reign yourself in. That's overspending.

Beauty products are often chic, status product areas for us debtors—we feel like we're really pampering ourselves by debting to buy them, and then we call the expenditures "needs." We're lying to ourselves. We can't afford these products. Our income is not proportional to the expense. The good news about beauty products is that there are many, many affordable knock-offs to fill our needs, either online, in drug stores, or in health food stores.

These days, I buy one nice lipstick for $14 and the rest I get for $3 at the local drug store. I've sworn off all department store and swanky products and use one jar of shea butter on my skin for $9 a month and body lotion for $6, which I buy online. And yes, yes, yes, I've heard all the hype about makeup color palettes and skincare "quality," and why it's so important to spend $49 on mascara or eye shadow—but let's be honest: This is an area where you can truly allot $25 a month and reasonably outfit yourself with enough products to fill your every need. You don't have to give up glam for solvency. You just give up the guilt.

VITAMINS

Buy in discount stores or buy cheaply online. Vitamins are another shopping addiction arena for debtors. We rifle through the health-food store or the herbal catalog and think, "Oooh, yes, COQ10—I read about that. And Pro-Biotics—must have that. And a nice Herbal Relaxation mix might be nice, and . . . and . . . and . . ." Here's a tip for buying vitamins: If you take them regularly, then give yourself a monthly allotment for them, buy them once at the beginning of the month, and let that amount service you for the entire month. If you run out in week two, then you're out until the next month.

Buying online will save you a lot of cash—and though it's great to support local stores when you can, when you're in debt that's not your job. Your job is to learn to live solvent, to get your goods and services for less than what you've been spending so you can live on cash and not on credit. I give myself $50 a month and buy once a month from online sites such as swansonsvitamins.com, herbproducts.com, or iherb.com—the best prices and quality I've found. But find your own sites—there are tons of them. Buy whatever your monthly allotment can get you each month (including shipping) and no more.

WAXING, HAIRCUTS, AND HAIR COLOR

Find affordable service providers or do your own. Working with clients has taught me one very important thing: There may be one expense in your Spending Plan that you are willing to pay a little more for just to get the quality you have found in one particular service provider. For many people, haircuts or waxing are often that Spending Plan item. And that's all fine and good *if the expense is proportional to your income*—that is, it needs to work in your Spending Plan.

If you're struggling along on $150 a month on food, then a $220 hairdresser each month is not in your realm of "proportional." If your after-bills income is $1,000 to cover all your needs, then $190 a month for bikini and brow waxing is just not reasonable. So what do you do to get the services you need? *You use your creativity to look for ways to get these needs met in less expensive ways.* Beauty schools are terrific places to get great haircuts, color, and styling for next to nothing. Often schools do waxing as well.

You may find a brilliant waxing aesthetician in a working-class neighborhood (versus a more affluent neighborhood), at prices half as much as what you've been paying. You may find a hair stylist who works out of his or her home, or you may be willing to do a $15 cut for a while—or possibly for every other cut. Here's the thing: Cutting the overpriced hairstylist and overspending on waxing will free up cash, and that's what you're after—more ingenuity to get your needs met and more cash to fund what's more meaningful to you long term. Wouldn't you rather have a paid-for-in-cash vacation instead of that overpriced waxing?

BODYWORK

Use only very affordable practitioners. Bodywork is a favorite debting area for those of us who are in over our heads. We're stressed because of our financial situation, and so we feel *entitled* to debt to get massages, chiropractic care, and acupuncture. We *need* it, we tell ourselves, because we're so stressed out. And somehow, we always manage to find the priciest practitioners—and then end up justifying our debting to pay for them. "He's the best. I know he's pricey, but I couldn't possibly work with anyone else."

Tell me how crazy this is. I debt, I get stressed out, I need bodywork to help me "unwind," and then I debt to pay for the bodywork, reigniting the cycle of debt and stress all over again. It's a black hole to go into debt for bodywork, so make a pledge right now to stop doing it.

When I worked on my own Debt-Free Spending Plan, I was willing to put a little more money into this category to make sure I had the care I needed. Very quickly I discovered that I could get all of the affordable treatments I needed at the local acupuncture school, where graduate residents worked on me for $39 a session. I could fit that cost into my Spending Plan, and I was willing to make it work so that I could have a treatment every week. Then I built in a monthly massage at a local massage school, and a category for occasional chiropractic care. Since I'm very physically active, this arena was a priority for me, and with a little ingenuity I was able to fund more than I thought I needed *in cash.*

That's the upshot of so much of what we're talking about: Use your creativity and ingenuity to cover more of your Daily Needs, and you will, I promise, have more money for the things you really, truly want.

CLOTHING

Shop at affordable stores and live within your monthly allotment of cash.
Clothing is a big debtor area for many of us. As debtors we tend to
(1) not plan for clothing expenses, and (2) overspend mindlessly
when we do purchase clothing.

It was a revelation to me when I was beginning my Debt-Free
Spending Plan to realize that clothing is a *need* and not a luxury. For
those of us who love clothing (and the buying of it), we think of new
clothes as a *reward*—a treat and a charm for feeling good about ourselves. When we debt to buy it, we have buyer hangover—a great,
almost giddy feeling for a day or two, and then we feel racked with
guilt for overspending. We have never set aside a reasonable amount
for the expenses of clothing on a monthly basis, so we feel guilt *every*
time we spend money on clothes. By using your Spending Plan, you
don't have to carry that weight around anymore.

For those of us who avoid buying clothing, the opposite is true:
We often hate shopping and will deprive ourselves for years, wearing
the same ratty shirts or shoes. This is also a debting issue. When we
do this, we debt against ourselves by not providing for our own
needs. Allotting reasonable amounts for your clothing encourages
you to spend money on the clothes you need, and that, in turn, lets
you know you're taking good care of yourself.

Everyone needs new socks, new underwear, and often new sneak-
ers every year. Many of us will need new sweaters, new shirts, new
jeans, or an outfit for an event or occasion. In other words, for those
of us for whom clothing is an overspending issue, *and* for those of us
who tend to deprive, we need to learn that regular purchases of
clothing support a healthy, provided-for life. (If clothing is a reward
for you, then feel free to use your Fun Money and your Clothing
money to purchase a "treat" for yourself. That's what it's there for.)

Lastly, clothing is an expense that will vary radically in price
points. We know good and well that buying T-shirts at the high-end
boutique will cost $90 compared to $15 at the discount store for the

same look. So shop wisely. Buy T-shirts, plain shirts and sweaters, underwear and bras—basics, in other words—in discount stores, and save for quality items that make your wardrobe work. (Swanky catalog lingerie stores with overpriced bras and undies are *out* for the moment, unless you have more than enough to make those purchases work in your Spending Plan.) If your affordability threshold is higher, and you're used to spending $800 or $1,200 on suits, but you're not paying back the note on the $165,000 you borrowed from your mother-in-law, then you are still out of proportion on your clothing purchases (and probably others).

Here's the basic rule of thumb: Give yourself a monthly allotment that works in your Spending Plan and stick to it. If you want to save for something special, take the cash out of your account and put it in an envelope so you can't touch it for anything else but your upcoming purchase. My promise to you is this: You will feel amazing about your new paid-for-in-cash clothing—and about yourself for buying with no guilt.

MEDICAL CO-PAYS

Plan your doctor visits, and save a stash for unexpected visits. One of the ways debtors continue to stay in debt is by not planning for the inevitable. So, while I can plan how many physical therapy appointments I may have in a month, I can't predict when I will get sick and need to visit my primary physician—or what meds I may need and how much of them will be covered by my insurance. If your co-pays are reasonable—say $15 to $35 a visit—you may be able to use money from your Short-Term Savings account to cover unexpected doctor visits. And you may need to do that if something goes wrong and you're at the doctor or clinic six or seven times in a month. Seven unexpected visits (or more) can really rock your Spending Plan.

My suggestion is this: In a month when you're not seeing the doctor, set aside your co-pay money in an envelope. (For me, that amount is $30 a month.) Then the next time you need a little extra, you can take it out of your medical co-pay stash and you will still stay solvent. And, once again, we always keep a Short-Term Savings account to cover our unexpected expenses.

AN ABSOLUTE NECESSITY

If you're not insured, get insured. The fastest way to drown in debt is to try to pay for medical care without insurance.

DENTAL WORK

Get clear quotes before dental services are provided, and obtain three contrasting quotes for all major work. Dental services can really mess up your Spending Plan. They are most often unexpected expenses, and dentists are famous for a sense of urgency in doing work that may, or may not, need to happen immediately. And we, as debtors, are famous for taking the bait and using credit to pay.

If you have a dental insurance plan, get clarity on how it works. In mine, I can be a "premier" patient (at $200 *less* per year in total services and 30 percent higher fees), or a "regular patient" (lower fees and more services) *at the same dentist.* I never would have known that I had a choice had I not called to check on the cost of my crowns, and I would have been charged the premier rate had I not gotten clarity and asked to be a "regular" patient.

In other words, ask questions and get clear numbers. How do you do that? First, by getting three comparison quotes; second, by getting a realistic time frame for when the work needs to get done. Tell your dentist *before* he or she works on you that you have a very strict Spending Plan and that you need to okay any extra costs before having the work done. For me, that means that my dentist knows that, even though she's working in my mouth and I'm numb and can barely talk, she still needs to get an okay from me about the extra cost of filling a neighboring cavity. There is nothing more empowering than telling people that they cannot overcharge you or randomly do work on you without your financial consent.

If you have a serious dental need and you have little cash to cover the expense, then go to a dental school. It will take longer, but it will cost one-half to one-third of commercial prices. There is always a way to cut the expense that used to tempt you to debt. And from here on out, you pay for everything in cash—even dental work.

CAR REPAIRS

Plan for car maintenance and have a savings account for unexpected car repairs. As debtors, our approach to car repairs is usually to fervently pray that nothing ever goes wrong and we never have to spend money on our cars—an exercise in futility, at best. When something does go wrong we feel put-upon, even oppressed, by the universe. This, it hardly needs saying, is not realistic.

Here's a basic rule that we use in our house: If our car is not under warranty, then we put away $80 a month in a Car Repairs Savings account. That's $960 a year for basic things that can go wrong on a car. This amount is not going to cover a new engine or a major body shop overhaul (which is why you need a Short-Term Savings account, too), but it will cover most of what you'll need in a year. Often we debtors drive beat-up cars and go into debt to fix them. If this is the case for you, start a new car fund, even if it's only $25 a month. Beginning to save for a cause will always change the course of your path, so start now.

GIFTS

Let your loved ones know that you're working to improve your finances, so all gifts will be small. Gifts are an amazingly complex emotional debting arena. It's your sister's birthday, and you run out and buy a $50 gift certificate or an expensive Ann Taylor blouse, debting to pay for it, and you convince yourself that you "had to."

As debtors, we already know our patterns around this issue: We overspend at Christmas and Hanukkah, we're unreasonable about overbuying for our spouse's fortieth, we think our son needs a new iPod, a new skateboard, *and* a new computer for his graduation. And, often when we take a hard look at our numbers, we can't afford any of these gifts. So what do we do? We don't want to stop giving—but over-giving is racking up both guilt and debt for us.

Here's what you can do. First, have a Spending Plan for gifts. Put aside $25 or $35 for holiday presents in a special Savings account. Build in $25 for family birthday gifts into your Spending Plan. Or write down all your important yearly birthdays and figure out how much you need each month and build that amount into your Spending Plan.

Most of us will expect that we can spend much more on gifts than we can afford. Know this: Your extra cash needs to go to you *first*, to the things that are meaningful to you, so you don't debt. So, the easiest way to eliminate all of that gift-debting is to tell your loved ones, "I'm working to improve my finances, and so all of my gifts are going to be small ones for a while."

My friends and I have had a blast exchanging less than $10 or less than $5 gifts at birthdays and holidays. We all stay solvent, and the pressure is off, so the whole gift-giving experience has become fun and light-hearted and creative.

CONTRIBUTIONS

Give up making contributions unless you're living debt-free. This suggestion will seem anathema to many who are steeped in the give-10-per-cent-no-matter-what school of spiritual thought. Let me say it as simply as I know how: *It is not a spiritual principle to debt in order to fund our favorite church, charity, or temple.*

Now, if you can bring your Spending Plan into alignment—meaning your cash can cover *all* of your needs, including reasonable Savings, Vacation, and Fun Money—then, by all means, give. Giving is a reward in and of itself. We know that. But here's what many of us debtors have been doing: We're contributing a good chunk of our cash to a cause, believing that somehow, because it's a charitable organization, it doesn't count as debt. And I have to say it right here: *Debt is debt.* It doesn't matter if it's for a spiritual charity, your kids' camp costs, or a binge in the Best Buy electronics department. If you're giving away the cash that you need to live, and then debting elsewhere to pay for needs, *that's a debt cycle.*

Many of us also make contributions to engage in magical thinking—meaning, we believe that if we give 10 percent, even if the actual dollar amount is not affordable, somehow a magic money tree will fall down from the sky and land in our bank account because we gave to a cause. We hear all of those childhood adages in our heads: "The money you give the church costs you nothing" or "To give is to receive." And I say this with due respect for the grace that I have received from being a part of spiritual groups and congregations: It is not right to debt for *anything* and then try to justify it by calling it a "spiritual experience." If you cannot afford your church or synagogue, find another one for a while. Give of your time, your expertise, or your energy for a while, until you're solvent again. Or give a small amount that you can easily fit into your Spending Plan. But do not gouge to give to a cause.

It is your first and foremost spiritual and health obligation, in my opinion, to live debt-free—which, by the way, promotes the spiritual principles of honesty, humility, service, and right-livelihood. As delicate a subject as this is for debtors, I believe it must be addressed. Our obligation, spiritually, is to make our contributions come into alignment with our proportional expenses. When we're in debt, that usually means giving much less cash—or none—to others, and much more to ourselves until we get solvent. Learning to live debt-free, in and of itself, is a huge, worthy, and blessed spiritual quest.

Making Cuts in Your Monthly Bills Categories

This section could easily be titled, "Some Pain-in-the-Butt Changes That You'll Want to Make Anyway." Once again, Bills are all the items you are charged for monthly, that you pay in the form of a check, automatic bank deduction, or online payment. These are things like phone bills, rent, mortgage, health insurance, movie subscriptions, gym memberships, newspaper subscriptions, monthly prescriptions (meds you take every day), and so on. Remember that you're going to go to any lengths to relieve yourself of money stress. So, if it seems intense to cut Bills, know that the debt stress of spiraling balances makes the intensity of cutting expenses look like a walk in the park.

Cutting your Bills takes a little more effort than cutting your Daily Needs, mainly because you already feel locked into these expenses. You're already paying for these bills (or trying to), so you think that you have to *keep* paying them. Not so. With a little bit of effort, you can relieve yourself of stress-producing bills that are outside of your proportional income range—that is, they are beyond your reasonable ability to pay them, based on what you're making. But you're going to have to be really, really honest with yourself.

Usually, our issue with out-of-proportion bills is our own ego: We want to keep deluding ourselves that whatever we're making payments on should continue to be ours, even if we genuinely cannot afford it. But it's what we cannot afford that has caused our insanity, our stress, and the dire circumstances of our finances. So we've got to be willing to look at more than just a few cuts in our Daily Needs spending. We've got to be willing and ready to pay off, sell, or give back the big-ticket items that we can't afford.

That's a big pill to swallow for most of us. So, be willing to tell yourself the truth about each and every item that follows, and imagine what the results of all this cutting will be. That is, you'll gain a feeling of peace with your money each and every month until the day you die. It means cash, not credit card balances, for the things that are truly meaningful to you. Paid-for Bills, paid-for Daily Needs, and paid-for wants *in cash*.

So, let's begin. Take each item one by one, and note whether or not you need to get a little more information (like comparison prices) or make cuts to free up cash. We'll address everything you can cut, from small-ticket to big-ticket items.

MOVIE SUBSCRIPTIONS

Cancel subscriptions or downsize to the cheapest plan. Most of us, these days, have a Netflix membership or some other version of a movie subscription sent to us or offered up via our computer. Though it may only be $20 a month, if you're in debt and overspending, and your first-pass Spending Plan is close to the bone, you're going to need that cash for Daily Needs. So just cancel it. Use the public library's collection of DVDs—they're free—or use a free, direct-streaming online service. (Free means free—no monthly fees.) It's not going to kill you to stop paying for movies for a while.

NEWSPAPER AND MAGAZINE SUBSCRIPTIONS

Cancel expensive subscriptions and read the publications online for free or at the library. Big *New York Times* fan? Love the *Wall Street Journal*, or maybe your local paper? Cancel it. Cut out the online service for $20, the hard-copy paper, *and* the $6.99 online access plan. Go to the library, read the papers at work, listen on TV or radio, or surf the Web for free news outlets, but don't run up debt to get your news when there are so many free ways to get it.

Remember, we're downsizing for a while to learn how to live debt-free. Once you've accomplished that, and you have a little extra in cash, then you can reconsider your news outlets. The same goes for magazines. If you want to allocate some of your Fun Money for a Sunday *New York Times*, then by all means, go to the store and buy it. But if you're in debt, get rid of the subscriptions.

GYM MEMBERSHIPS

Cancel the swanky gym membership and find a cheaper one. With the advent of the spa-motif, gym memberships have become as swanky as four-star hotels. But if you're in debt, you can't afford the swanky gym right now and you know it. Let's say your after-Bills money is $750 a month, and that's got to cover all of your Daily Needs, Savings, and Fun Money. You're going to have to downsize to live on your income anyway, so you definitely can't afford $125 a month for a gym membership. Or let's say your after-Bills money is $2,000, but you're funding a whole family on that cash. You can deceive yourself into thinking that the $125 is a small portion of your $2,000, but if it is needed to fund a family of four, your swanky gym membership has to go. Your expenses must be proportional to your income.

I've worked out in gyms all my life—the gritty ones and the luxe ones—and at the end of the day, a gym's a gym. So just nix the excuses: "But my gym's so *clean*" (a gym is a sweat factory; "clean gym" is an oxymoron); "It's so close to my house" (so bike to the cheaper one, and get a few more miles in on your exercise routine); "I only do yoga with one teacher" (then you'll have to get used to a new one). We don't like change, granted. But here's the news flash: You don't get to run up debt or gouge your expenses to keep your gym.

Either find a cheap gym that works in your Spending Plan, or buy yourself a couple of workout DVDs and exercise at home for a while. When I was working my Spending Plan for the first time and was out of work, I got a scholarship at the YMCA, drove a few blocks farther, and parked on the street instead of using the pay lot—and saved myself $75 a month. Do what you need to, but if you're in debt, swanky gyms are out.

SMARTPHONES

Keep your current phone and don't even shop for a new one. You know and I know that this has just got to stop. Buying a new phone and service plan every time a manufacturer comes out with a new gadget is a ridiculously easy way to debt. Keep your current plan if it's reasonable, and keep your current phone. If it's Christmas or Hanukkah, and you've saved up your cash for a new one, then go for it. But only if you can afford the new plan that accompanies it *in cash* without depriving your other needs. Can I tell you how many debtors I've worked with who have Cadillac smartphones and not enough for monthly dry cleaning?

PHONE PLANS

Get three contrasting quotes for phone plans and buy what's most affordable. Most of us are paying too much for too many services. Get rid of high-cost phone providers. Get three contrasting quotes, and pick the one that's most affordable. Use your home phone more than your mobile if you have trouble going over your minutes. If you do go over on minutes month after month, then buy a phone with a monthly limited amount—one that turns off automatically when the minutes are up. Always, always, always investigate a plan that better serves your calling needs if you keep going over. Look at your statement and see if your minutes are reasonable—if not, get a plan that covers your actual usage and make it work in your Spending Plan. Don't debt to pay for overage fees—that's just silly.

If you're living on very, very little, then keep a cheap cell plan and get rid of your home phone—or vice versa: lose the cell phone altogether, if that's your overspending culprit. We all lived without two phones before the invention of the cell, so if you're an abuser of your phone bill, then get rid of the temptation to mindlessly run up expenses in this area. If you can't stay within your minutes even after you've adjusted your service plan, then—honest to God—get rid of the cell phone.

CABLE

Cancel the cable and rent for free from the library for a while. This expense will generally be the one item that sends debtors over the edge at the very whisper of living without it. *Cancel my cable? Are you out of your mind?* Once again, I don't get to tell you what to cut and what not to—you're the adult, and you get to choose. But you also must cover all of your Bills and Daily Needs in cash, with no credit. That's the deal. So, if you're paying $120 for a cable package with all the premium channels because you *need* it, but your groceries category is only $150 a month and you're feeding two people on that money, I can tell you right now that you can't afford the cable. You're depriving yourself in the food category and probably some others; and cable is not—no, it's not—a necessity. These days, with free streaming options, all you need is a $40 cable to connect your computer to your TV, and you'll get everything your cable service has to offer, for free.

Here's the upshot: If your after-Bills money doesn't offer you enough cash to reasonably cover food, fuel, dry cleaning, drug store items, clothing, household stuff, kids' allowance, and all the things you need to live, *and* leave you some cash for Fun and Savings, then—sorry—you can't afford cable. Cancel it, use the DVDs at the library for free for a while, or use free streaming services until you're living debt-free and can afford it again.

CAR INSURANCE

Compare prices and buy what's most affordable, billed monthly. Once again, get three contrasting quotes to see if you're paying too much. Make sure you're getting all the discounts that apply: good driver, married, weekend driver, whatever. Ask to review what the company's discounts are. Make sure your new company will bill you monthly (not quarterly or semi-annually). Your goal is to have complete clarity on what your monthly expenses are, and to pay as many as possible on a monthly basis so there are few or no other Bills to save for. When everything's covered monthly, you keep your extra cash.

APPLIANCES, FURNITURE, AND COMPUTERS

Only buy when you truly need a new item, and then save, shop around, and get three comparison quotes before purchasing. Bought that mega chef-quality stove, and now you realize you can't afford it? Bought the most expensive computer (plus accessories) at your local electronics store, and now the monthly amount is cutting into your expense needs? Spent $8,000 on a leather couch, and the monthly payment is killing you? *Then sell it and buy something cheaper.* If you financed the thing for five years and you've only got a year left, then pay it off if you can. But if you're still paying interest and the monthly is gouging your Daily Needs, Bills, and Savings money, just sell it. Buy something you can purchase with cash—something that works and something you can afford. Do *not* go into debt for a cheaper model. Remember that we're going to any length to get free of debt, so we're not going to sell and rebuy on credit. We don't use credit ever again, except for a secured home or car loan. That's it.

HEALTH INSURANCE

Get three quotes and buy the most affordable plan—one that covers more of your annual needs. If you're paying for health insurance yourself, do the same thing as you did for obtaining car insurance. If your employer pays for your health insurance, and you have a choice of plans, review the costs and choose whichever one is cheapest for a while. No whining about providers and PPOs. Get an affordable plan, even if it means switching to the cheapest HMO, even if it means getting a new doctor for a while. It's not for forever, and you can't afford the Cadillac plan right now anyway, so get yourself off of it.

A note about high-deductible plans: These plans are especially tempting to debtors—we're gambling that we won't have to use the plan. But this is not wise. Since most of us don't have any savings when we agree to stop debting, and since we are just beginning to build reserves for things like medical expenses, we need a health plan that covers our actual medical needs as completely as possible. We don't want to set ourselves up for tripping potentially large land-mines, and we don't debt anymore—not even for medical care. So my advice is to pay for the most reasonable plan that covers as much of your yearly medical costs and major medical insurance as possible. We need to know what our medical care will cost us, all the way through the year. No gambling please.

HEALTH SAVINGS ACCOUNTS AND MEDICAL SAVINGS PLANS

Use a Health Savings Account (HSA) for as many health-care expenses as you can. Health Savings Accounts are a terrific tool that can help you plan for health-care costs—and do so tax-free. Here's how they work: The IRS currently allows us up to $3,100 in contributions to a Health Savings Account per year per individual, which can then be used for medical costs such as co-pays, health plan deductibles, uncovered health-care services, and some medical supplies. Families can contribute up to $6,250. Set up an HSA account with a qualifying bank and make monthly contributions, proportional to your Spending Plan. Because the money is contributed pre-tax, your net income may vary only slightly after the contribution.

Many employers now offer company-sponsored Medical Savings Plans, and will often automatically deduct pre-tax contributions from your paycheck. Check with your administrator or accountant to see if you qualify for either a Medical Savings Plan or a Health Savings Account. If you do not spend all the money contributed each year in an HSA, the cash stays in the account as interest-accruing savings that you can use for any qualifying cost later on. Medical Savings Plans, however, sometimes require you to use the entire amount contributed in a year, or you lose the overages. So, get clarity before you contribute, both on the amounts you will need and the terms of the Medical Savings Plan. (I currently use First American Bank for my HSA, since their fees are the lowest I've found, but there are dozens of financial institutions that sponsor them; see www.firstambank.com.)

MEDICATIONS

Buy generic and don't whine about it. As noted in the construction of your Debt-Free Spending Plan, you include as a Bill any monthly medications that you pay for at the first of the month—things like blood pressure meds or birth control pills—which are daily doses that are paid for each month. The most obvious way to reduce medication costs is to buy generic. It doesn't matter that you think the brand name is "better." If you're in debt and trying to learn to live without debting, then you're buying generic, period.

I've had clients who were paying over $1,000 a month for name-brand medications, were uninsured, and were debting to pay for them. So, if you need regular meds, shop around for a reasonable insurance plan (three quotes) or get a job that covers you and your family. Don't gouge your living expenses by not taking care of the things that need attention. Pay attention and do what needs to be done.

CAR PAYMENTS

Buy reasonable, affordable vehicles. Sell any car that you can't afford. We debtors are very fond of buying cars we cannot afford. We're in a BMW, but we can't pay our bills on time; we've got a new Toyota Tundra truck, but we can't make our child support payments. Stop it.

You don't get to buy a new car until you (1) have saved the down payment in cash, and (2) can pay *all* your Bills and Daily Needs, and still have enough left over to easily cover that monthly new car note. So, what do you do if you're paying $550 on a car loan and it's seriously eating into your monthly Debt-Free Spending Plan? Take steps to sell the car and get something cheaper, that's what. *You want me to sell my car? There's absolutely no way I'm doing that!*

What I'm saying is this: If you can't pay for your Bills and Daily Needs with ease on what you're making, then you have no business depriving yourself on food, clothes, child support, and other necessary expenses—even on Fun Money—so you can drive something that's newer or cooler. That's debting, and you're literally stealing from your own and your families' needs by doing it. We have got to get this through our heads: If we can't afford it, we can't have it.

RENT AND MORTGAGE

Be willing to change your housing arrangements if you cannot afford where you live. If you're in a house or an apartment that you can't afford, be willing to take a look at what that's doing to the quality of your life. The same thing that is true for your car applies here: You have no business being in an apartment or house that gouges your monthly living expenses to the point where you feel compelled to debt to live. Obviously, a reduction in housing expenses is a major investment in effort, but if you need to look under that rock and make some changes, be willing to.

If you've got a subprime loan, an upcoming balloon that you can't pay, *and you're in serious credit card and credit line debt,* then you need to face the music. You need to find housing that you can afford. I'm not saying you shouldn't try to keep your house if it's reasonable. What I am saying is that if you could never afford it in the first place, and now you're debting to live—both in your housing expense and your living expenses—or if your income has dropped significantly and you can no longer afford your house, then it's time to *move.*

So what's "reasonable"? Reasonable housing costs are proportional to your take-home income. Reasonable housing costs give you plenty to live on after you pay your house note or rent. And who cares that you're *used to* your house, or that you don't think you should have to move? If your housing costs are a major source of stress for you, then it's time to address them. What difference does it make if you're afraid your friends will marginalize you for moving from a house to an affordable apartment? It's not *their* stress levels we're talking about here. Your friends' opinions do not comfort you in the night when your blood pressure's up and you're worried sick about your debts.

Start Simply and Incrementally

If you've got shell shock right about now from the wake-up call of realizing that you need to cut some Bills and Daily Needs, then you're not alone. Most of us freak out when we realize just how much effort it's going to take to unload the ten-ton debtor rock that we've been carrying around on our backs. So start simply. Cut your Daily Needs expenses first, and make adjustments to your Debt-Free Spending Plan and record everything in your Magic Little Notebook. Then, start tackling your Bills reductions.

My advice is to investigate one Bill per week. If your phone plan is overpriced, then spend a couple of hours comparing three new plans and get the new, cheaper one under way. Here's one absolute rule: *Do not go into debt to get a cheaper plan, subscription, gym membership, computer, or anything else.* No high-end start-up fees that cause you to debt. There's no justifying a cheaper purchase by debting for it.

Then, the following week, take on your car insurance, making sure to get a monthly automatic deduction rather than a quarterly or annual bill. Go from small to large. In the very first week, make all the cancellations you need to make: newspapers, expensive movie subscriptions, magazines, cable—whatever it is that is not in line with your cash income. Then, week by week, address your remaining Bills, cutting and reducing where appropriate. Yes, it's a bit of work. But when you're sitting in Costa Rica, sipping a margarita, knowing your whole fourteen-day vacation there is covered in cash, you won't care that it took a few hours to cut some Bills to more manageable amounts.

6

. . . . .

Nailing Down the Octopus Arms

How to Pay Back Your Debts without Gouging Your Living Expenses

MULTIPLE DEBTS are like octopus arms—once we grab hold of one and slam it to the turf, another one pops up and smacks us in the head, demanding to be dealt with. For some of us, we have often ignored or avoided the disaster of multiple debts for so long that now we don't even look at or pay our bills. Even if we are still paying, managing the payments of, say, eight or nine creditors (often by dubious means), we often feel like we're riding on a train that's about to run off the tracks at any moment, crashing headlong into a ditch.

Sitting down to pay our creditors is an exercise in self-abuse: We sweat, we get angry, we feel sick to our stomachs, we break out in hives, we overeat, and after all of that, we just end up feeling hopeless. We think: *How in God's name am I ever going to get a grip on all of this?* It feels just like trying to hold down eight octopus arms—we wrestle one out-of-control, flinging arm to the ground, and—thwack!—we get slammed by another one.

Multiple debts are nasty that way. Even when we have pushed them to the dark corners of our consciousness, they return like bad dreams to hover over us and haunt us in the night. And if they have gone unaddressed for a long time (meaning, unpaid), they start multiplying in our minds. We feel as if there are an endless number of them—and that in and of itself can make us want to junk the whole damn carload of "owing" and escape, with tires screeching, to Bogotá.

ONE STEP AT A TIME

If you relegate every dime you have to debt repayment at this early stage, you will—I guarantee you—deprive yourself of your life necessities, and that will tempt you to debt again. *How come?* Because when you don't take care of your needs with the income you have, you feel rebellious and angry that your needs are not being met, and you will act out with your credit cards. You feel entitled to do that—and rightly so.

Right now, your focus has to be on *learning how to live well on what you earn*, on what you bring in. If you try to do everything at once—stop using credit cards, learn to live on the cash you bring in, *and pay off all of your debts as fast as possible*—it can overwhelm you. It *will* overwhelm you. How could it not? That's why this debt-repayment approach is incremental.

But do not despair. Your strategy in dealing with multiple debts is going to be simple, easy, and straightforward. Here's what you will do: You will nail down all of the octopus arms of your debts, one by one, until each one is addressed. You will, one at a time, develop a plan to deal with every one of them until—you guessed it—they are all securely nailed down to the turf.

So what does "addressed" mean? Am I going to have to live on chicken broth and crackers? No. Nailing down the flailing arms of your debts does not mean paying back what you owe all at once. It does not mean killing yourself with three jobs to get out from under the weight of it all. It does not mean starving and scrimping to live for your creditors. Nailing down the octopus arms of your debts means creating a Debt-Repayment Plan—a payback amount for each debt that does not gouge your living expenses, and is reasonable in relation to your needs. In other words, *you're going to employ the same proportional rule for your debts as you used for your Daily Needs and your Bills.* You are going to pay what is proportional and reasonable in relation to your income, without depriving yourself on your living expenses.

I know, I know—you don't believe that this is possible. You're worried about your credit rating. You've somehow managed to pay your minimums—though it's killing your ability to live on what you're making—and you're still debting, right? I've been there, too. If things are bad, you've got five credit cards maxed out at $20,000 each and you can barely cover your monthly expenses before addressing debt repayment. Or, your consulting income has dropped in half and you're at bare bones just covering the minimums on only two of your creditor payments, let alone your unaddressed IRS debt. Or, you've been moving money from card to card, and you can't pay the minimums on any of them if you stop the roulette. We've all been there in one form or another.

And, once again, you're still going to look at what's reasonable and proportional. You're still going to create a Debt-Repayment Plan.

The Value of a Debt-Repayment Plan

A Debt-Repayment Plan is just what it sounds like: It's a list of everything you owe, and an amount noted to pay back each month against the debt. If you've been living way beyond your means for a long time—or project debting for a business or a creative venture as I did, running up lots of debt fast—then your list is going to be long. But it doesn't matter how long it is, or even how much it is. You're going to come up with reasonable, monthly debt-repayment amounts in relation to your income, and once that Debt-Repayment Plan is in motion, *you're going to forget about your debts for a while and concentrate on learning how to use your Debt-Free Spending Plan to live well on the cash you have.*

In other words, for now, you're going to pay your minimums if you can and let the debts alone for a while. You won't stress about how you'll pay back the $85,000 in credit card debt at $450 a month in payments. You're going to address it with a payment amount each month, and then you're going to *leave it be.*

IF YOU CAN'T PAY YOUR MINIMUMS

I don't need to spell out for you how monthly minimums can drain your energy for living. You and I both know that if you're in over your head, the minimums are going to more than likely catch up with you and wreck your ability to live on the cash you earn.

So what do you do if you owe seven creditors somewhere between $165 and $275 each a month? What if your total minimums to creditors are $500, $700, or even $1,000 a month and your after-bills money is $1,200 or less? What if you're making good money—say, $200,000 or more—but your monthly minimums are as high as $4,000 a month? If you're playing roulette, moving money from credit card to credit card to pay these minimums, and you still feel like you're barely making it, how can you stop the madness?

Here's how: You're going to stop paying the *full amount* of your minimums. You're going to contact your creditors and tell them why. And you're going to craft a Debt-Repayment Plan to pay them back *something* each month—even if it's only $5 per creditor. Now, you may think what I'm saying is irresponsible, or financially unsound, or out of the realm of the possible—but it's not. You *can* stop paying your minimums and stay in good standing with your creditors. You may think I'm advocating the fall of the American credit industry. You may think I'm saying you can get away with not paying and then keep debting. I'm not. I *am* advocating that you stop the roller-coaster of debt creation by being honest about what it costs you to live, what you need to do to live within your means, and what is reasonable to pay back, given that you no longer incur debt.

Get it? This is the point where you really have to ask yourself, *Has my behavior changed? Am I willing to say that I will never use credit cards or credit lines to live again? Can I honestly say that I have reached the lowest point I ever want to descend to, and that my new Debt-Free Spending Plan marks the new debt-free life I am embarking on?* If you can, then you can stop stressing about your minimums and develop a plan to pay back debts that will let you live on your cash. Let that effort be enough until you're on more solid ground.

In his book *The One Minute Apology*, Kenneth H. Blanchard advocates a very powerful principle that can help us all with our debting issues. Blanchard says that "Our amends are made in changed behavior." In other words, "I'm sorry" all by itself is just not going to work here; it's our changed behavior that makes the apology real.

So, we don't get to stop paying our creditors and keep running up debt. But if we truly are changing our behavior to live debt-free—a path we're committed to for the rest of our lives—and we've cut up our credit cards and have canceled all the accounts, then it makes sense to bring our monthly debt amounts into an honest realm. Yes, we made the mistake of getting ourselves into debt. But the way out is not to keep moving money from credit card to credit card. The way out is to *stop*. And in order to stop, we may have to pay less than our minimums.

HOW DO I BEGIN DEBT REPAYMENT?

So, how do we craft a Debt-Repayment Plan? How can we tell how much to pay and how much is too much to pay back?

First things first. When you begin your Debt-Free Spending Plan, you are likely to underestimate at least some of the spending areas in your Spending Plan. So, know that in the first few months of your Spending Plan, you will be adjusting it to see what you really need. That means you need to be *flexible*. It may take two to three months before you're clear about what really works in your food, fuel, clothing, and other categories, and what you can reasonably allocate for debt repayment.

So, just do the best you can in the first month, and as your Daily Needs become clear to you, adjust to meet them. That means that if you have set aside $394 a month for a lump-sum debt repayment, and you find that you're running out of food money by the second week of the month and there's no place else to adjust your Spending Plan, then you may have to pay less on debt repayment to fund your Daily Needs.

Easy-Does-It Payback Plans

Here's how to craft your Debt-Repayment Plan. At the bottom of your Spending Plan, or on a separate document, simply list all of your debts. (If you're already paying on your debts, then your monthly payments will be listed under your Bills section in your Debt-Free Spending Plan.) Now, list what you owe, in total, for each debt.

Don't freak out here, or start hyperventilating. For now, they're just numbers. For now, be consoled by the fact that you're starting a whole new chapter in your financial life. But get it down on paper. It looks like this.

Card/Credit Line	Amount	Minimum Reasonable Payback Amount
Bank of America Card	22,375.13	321.09
Chase Visa	14,102.11	165.77
Dividend Miles Master Card	5,432.09	102.00
Cal State Long Beach Visa	2,987.74	65.71
Best Buy	2,887.45	59.02

Gap	789.44	39.77
Kohl's	459.06	22.19
Total		775.55

The most important sum in this table is not your total debt owed to all your creditors. The most important number is the minimum payments you owe each month. That's what we're after here. Do not take this opportunity to emotionally beat yourself up by adding your total debt and then creating a deep, dark depression in your heart.

Yes, it's absolutely tempting to wallow in thinking, *Oh, my God. How did I do this to myself?* But it's not useful. That was then; this is now. Then, you were debting. Now, you're learning to live debt-free. You're reading this book. You're developing this Debt-Repayment Plan. You're taking steps to improve your situation. And though it may feel like you're climbing a mountain top that looks totally, impossibly steep just now, you will still get to the top, by taking one solid step at a time. So just breathe and pace yourself, step by step.

PAY YOUR MINIMUMS IF YOU CAN

To determine how much to pay your creditors, go back to your Debt-Free Spending Plan and see how much it realistically costs you to live. If you have $775.55 in credit card minimums, and after paying those minimums, plus your regular bills, you have $1,200 or $2,000 or so to cover your Daily Needs, then you may well be able to cover all of your minimum payments. You will creatively fund your daily living expenses and keep in good standing with your creditors.

In other words, if you can pay your minimums, do it—and then leave the bills alone for a while. Don't stress over when they will be paid off. Just live within your means for a time. Get that skill under your belt. And, as time progresses, you can determine whether you want to allocate more money to debt repayment. Remember: If you do nothing else besides live within your means—meaning live on *cash*—you will eventually pay off your debt. It may take some time, but if you're not adding to the balances, it will eventually get paid off and go away.

BUT WHAT IF I CAN'T?

What if your credit card payments are $775.55 a month and that leaves only $224.45 in after-Bills money—meaning $224.45 would have to cover all of your Daily Needs? It's pretty obvious that that won't work. No one can reasonably live on $224.45 and still pay for food, fuel, dry cleaning, savings, or entertainment—on that amount of money. The $224.45 is not nearly enough to live on for all of the Daily Needs that come up in a month.

So, you have to allocate enough for your Daily Needs, and then allot what is reasonable, after that, to debt repayment. In this instance, it's probably not going to be much. But you always pay *something* and keep yourself in good standing with your creditors— and you always stay in communication with them (see below). That way, you keep your integrity until things improve financially and you can pay more.

Credit Ratings and Less Than Minimum Monthly Payments

If you're having a panic attack over what all of this is going to mean for your credit rating, you are not alone. All of us who could not pay our minimums have had the same wake-up call about our credit ratings. When I was $80,000 in debt and playing credit-card roulette— sick to my stomach every day over my situation—my credit rating was still just dandy. A++. In other words, my credit rating was in no way an accurate portrayal of my well-being financially.

So let's clear something up: If you have been paying minimums by moving money from credit line to credit line, then your credit rating is not really accurate. In fact, it's a lie. I know we don't like hearing it, but paying one card with another to keep a credit rating is, indeed, lying. Truly, we're creating *more* debt, *more* stress, *more* of some kind of a vaporous pyramid-like scheme for ourselves and our families, and it's not honest. It does not breed peace and serenity. It does not help us sleep at night or look ourselves in the mirror in the morning.

Stressing about our credit ratings when we're still debting and over-spending, and can't pay our minimums, is like worrying about the hole in our umbrella when the flood has covered our house. And the only way to stop the insanity is to do just that: *Stop it* and face the music. That's what this whole Debt-Free Spending Plan is about—allowing ourselves, finally, to look at what we have and what we can spend, and then put the whole nightmare of living beyond our means to rest.

So, though it seems that the sky will fall when you pay less than your minimums and dink your credit rating, it will not. You will build it back up, with integrity, over time, as you stop debting and start living within your means.

How to Talk to Creditors

Let's say you're in a situation very near the example listed above. You've got $1,000 to live on after paying your regular, living-expense Bills, and you've got about $775.55 in credit card minimums each month. You know you can't pay $775.55 and still cover all of your Daily Needs on $224.45. So, how do you handle paying less than your minimums with your creditors?

Let's say you've decided to pay $10 a month per debt—a total of $70 for seven creditors. How do you approach them? What in God's name do you say?

Remember that what I'm offering here is a suggestion from my own and my clients' lives. Take what you like and leave the rest. Make it work for you, for your own, unique situation. This is what has worked for me, and for many others. But, again, it's your call.

THE WAKE-UP CALL

One day, when I was deep in debt, I woke up and realized that I could no longer pay my minimums if I was going to live debt-free.

It was a knock on the head by a two-by-four that I never saw coming. Yet, of course, the two-by-four had been aiming for my head for months and months; I had just chosen not to see it coming. I had been juggling credit cards, moving money from card to card to pay minimums, and waiting for some kind of miracle to bail me out. When my wake-up call finally came, my business was tanking and I knew I couldn't keep the balls in the air anymore. I admitted it: I was going to have to stop paying creditors in order to just survive. Yet I had no desire to have those harrowing late-night or early-morning phone calls from antagonistic creditors. I'd heard about them from my debtor friends, several of whom had become petrified to answer their own phones. I did not want to be a prisoner in my house, frightened to hear the telephone ring.

So, I wrote a letter *each month* with my $5 or $10 payment. I kept track of every date I sent a letter and I kept copies. I *called* them every month—keeping a list of the date and time I called and who I spoke with. That way, when I got the inevitable "Can you pay more?" call, or when the debt went to collections, I had a record of all my communications with my creditors. I used a script on the phone so I wouldn't stammer:

> Hi, Julie. Thanks for taking my call today. I'm calling to let you know that I am going to be paying less than my minimum this month. I'm going to be honest with you and tell you that I've gotten myself into debt trouble and I cannot pay my minimums and live within my means. I'm committed to paying you each and every month, and as things improve financially, I will attempt to make larger payments. For now $10 is all I can reasonably afford and still pay for rent, food, utilities, and basic living expenses.

Should you choose to do this, you'll find that Julie, the credit card company customer service representative, will probably try to coach you into paying more. I had one bank rep try to push me into paying my card off by running up debt on another card. *Don't fall for this.* Hold your ground. Simply say, "I have a very clear Spending Plan, I now live debt-free, and I won't be charging anything ever again. Right now, this is the total amount I can pay in my financial situation."

Be humble. Be gracious. Do not, under any circumstances, raise your voice. If the creditor representative raises his or her voice, get off the phone immediately. Say something like, "I am calling as a courtesy, but I can't stay on the phone if you raise your voice. Goodbye."

No phone-slamming. No abrupt rudeness. Be kind to your creditors, and ask for their understanding. Do not get huffy. They loaned you money, and you can't pay it back. So don't blame them or be rude to them. Just tell the truth as best you can and as humbly as you can.

Recognize that there is a human being on the other end of the line who has potentially had trouble with money and debt, too. Be respectful and take responsibility for your situation. And, of course, be reasonable with the amounts you can pay. Do not let yourself be talked into paying $100 a month when you can reasonably only pay $10. Have the utmost clarity about your numbers before you call your creditors, and be kind, every time.

One last thing: Make these calls *brief*—one to three minutes, tops. Back your call up with a letter that says basically the same thing you said verbally and attach your payment to it.

"THINGS WILL GET BETTER SOON"

When I was paying $5 per creditor to eight institutions, I was terrified of getting a rude bank rep on the phone. By following this strategy, I never had even one negative encounter. Some of the reps even said they would pray for me! Many encouraged me and said things like, "Don't worry. Things will get better for you soon."

JUSTIFYING THE LESS THAN MINIMUM REPAYMENT APPROACH

Paying less than our monthly minimums is a strategy for those of us who have "hit bottom" with our debts and are *finished* with credit card and credit line use. It's for those of us who have had enough of the disastrous stress that debt produces in our lives, and are now ready to go to whatever lengths we need to get free of it. It's for those of us who are now committed to living within our means and being honest about it—both to ourselves and to our creditors.

So it should be very clear to us that we cannot justify not paying our minimums if we're still out running up debt on other cards and credit lines. We don't get to use this as a gaming strategy to keep the balls in the air just a little longer. The question we might want to ask ourselves is this: *How low do I have to go before I change? Do I have to lose everything, including my relationships, before I stop debting?*

Remember the Kenneth Blanchard adage: "Our amends are made in changed behavior." *Changed behavior* means, first, that we stop debting. We cut up, cancel, or freeze all of our credit cards and credit lines. Second, we use the Debt-Free Spending Plan to learn to live within our means. Third, on the Debt-Repayment Plan, we list every creditor we owe money to and pay them back something every month. We do not lie, we do not hype our credit rating by moving money from card to card, and we do not stop paying creditors and keep debting. We make an honest start at a new financial life and we start now.

A Note About "Forgotten" Debts

When you're beginning to construct your Debt-Repayment Plan, you will likely "forget" about one, or even several, debts. You may list what you owe in your Debt Repayment Plan, and then a month later remember that you also owe your father $85,000 and haven't been paying it back. You're feeling really great about your debt-free efforts, and then you're suddenly struck by the remembrance that you owe back taxes of $30,000. You've listed all of your credit card debt, but you've spaced out on the $5,000 you owe the contractor you used to rebuild the garage.

Know that this happens to all of us. We all "forget" debts that we haven't been paying, debts that we've relegated to the back corners of our mind because we have no idea how we're going to pay for them—or we don't want to.

You may be tempted to despair when you wake up one morning, just two months into working your Spending Plan, and remember that you owe the musician who accompanied your movie $2,000 or you never paid your mother back the $4,500 you borrowed for the engine rebuild on your car. This is the moment to remember that the Debt-Free Spending Plan is a flexible tool. When expenses go up, you adjust. You take a little out of each spending category to make up for the added expense, and your plan still works for you. *You just adjust the numbers.* It truly is not rocket science.

Making Your Peace with the Payback Timeline

There are two things to be aware of when addressing your multiple debts:

1. There are a limited number of creditors you owe money to.

2. You are not alone.

All of us who have had multiple debts when we began our Debt-Free Spending Plan have thought that we'd never see the financial light of day. And all of us who have followed the Spending Plan have gotten relief. There are *not* an endless number of debts you owe. And because that number is limited, *and you're not adding to those balances anymore by debting*, you can, over time, make progress on paying down your debts.

In other words, if you stop debting, live on cash, *and* pay a reasonable amount to your creditors, you will, eventually, make all of your debts go away. Meaning, one day very soon you will be eating the very last arm of a dead and sautéed octopus. And it will be delicious.

7

. . . . .

Our Aphrodisiac Spending Plan

A Loving Approach to Approaching the One You Love about Debt Problems

SO MANY OF us have had trouble with money in our relationships that we've developed a sociological shorthand to describe our financial issues. That is, we dodge ("Every marriage has money trouble"), punt ("My partner is out of control with money"), or ignore ("We'll address it one of these days, but it's just too insane to look at right now").

We may even be brazen about it, speaking with casual abandon about our money troubles at parties or social events ("We're going to die in debt up to our eyeballs, and that's just the way it is"). But when it comes to honestly addressing our debt as a couple, many of us are shut down. We've developed coping skills by juggling (usually by ignoring) whatever balls we have in the air financially. Even when we're holding on by the skin of our teeth, both financially and as a couple, we persist in our heads-in-the-sand approach. We think our fights are our partner's fault, and when we do discuss money, we often erupt into blame over our heightened financial stress levels.

So the first thing that we need to do is to wake up to our *shared responsibility* in our financial mess. We may have an entire, spinning story about how we're not the one to blame, how our partner is the overspender, and how we have remained the neutral observer in our financial disasters. But blaming and shaming never helped solve anything. Blame doesn't change the situation; it just digs us a deeper hole. So if we're stacking up instances of our partner's fault in derailing our finances, standing on the sidelines with our army of righteous warriors ("My therapist says you're acting like a child!" "My father says you've never understood money!" "Our accountant says you're not earning enough!"), then we are truly not being honest with ourselves or our partner.

If there's a problem, and my partner and I have a tacit agreement to not discuss it unless someone blows up, or we have some sort of death-grip agreement to not bring it up until we both crash and burn, then guess what? *I am the other half of the problem.* Neither one of us has had the courage to address the matter head-on, in a calm manner, laying it all out on the table for viewing and discussion.

So, right now, before you read another sentence, make an agreement with yourself:

I will address what is happening now, what needs to be looked at as a couple. I will not wallow in blame or shame, or dwell on instances of what has happened in the past. I will be willing to start from today and craft a new financial road with my partner.

This goes back to our earlier discussion in Chapter 1 ("So, What Have I Been Spending, Anyway?") about digging up all of your past financial challenges, or trying to balance six months of previously unaddressed bank statements. Don't do it. *Just have clarity for today.* What that means is that you accept what already is—no matter what the damage level—and start from today to craft a new Debt-Free Spending Plan that will bring you both solvency and financial peace.

Lay the Unresolved Issue on the Table

For most of us in marriages or partnerships, the crux of our money problems is that we can't talk about them. Or, when we try, we just end up fighting, so we ignore the issue. We stuff it until we can't stand it another moment, then blow up, or snippily address each other, or psychoanalyze our partner as if we were the innocent in the situation. Those of us who can't speak up at all about money issues usually resort to resentment, to withholding, or to low-level biting behavior. Those of us who like to solve problems may resort to strategizing about what our partner should do (without addressing *our* part), approaching him or her with an I'm-the-authority attitude.

These are all poor communication strategies in partnerships when discussing money—or anything else, for that matter. Here's the challenge of dealing with money issues in a relationship: *You have to be willing to put the unresolved issue on the table and look at it, bare and without an answer.*

Our pop-psychology culture has left us with a codependent hangover that pains our relationships—that is, we think we're supposed to know the fix-it solution to problems before we openly discuss them. In fact, we're so afraid of uncertainty in our relationships—so terrified that problems mean the dissolution of the union—that we avoid letting the unsolved problem sit there so we can size up its dimensions, feel what we feel, and then proceed thoughtfully. So my suggestion is simple: When you begin to address money issues with your partner, don't come to the table with all of the answers. In fact, don't come with any answers. Just open up the topic for viewing, discussing, and pondering.

That said, this approach is not an excuse for not dealing with the problem. You're not looking for vagueness here. What you're looking for is a simple statement that lets your partner know that you can't keep living like this, that you realize there's a problem and that it's a serious one, and that you are committed to looking at it and creating a strategy for solving that problem.

THREE BIRDS TO CHANGE A PARADIGM

I had an acting coach in Los Angeles who used a terrific example of the progress of the human heart in accepting what it doesn't want to accept. It goes like this: You're sitting in the dining room of a well-appointed house, having a formal dinner, and you think you see a bird flit by on the ceiling. "Naw," you say to yourself, "can't be. I'm in the dining room. That couldn't have been a bird." You dismiss it, check how much wine you've drunk, and go on chatting with your neighbor. A few minutes later—flit!—there it is again! A bird flew through the dining room!

You look around and no one else seems to have noticed it. Everyone is still steadily talking as if nothing happened. You stop and say to the person next to you, "This is crazy, but did you see a bird in here a second ago?" Your neighbor looks at you incredulously, as if you're not quite stable.

"No birds in here, Jo. You all right?" A few minutes later—flit, flit!—there it is again. You *know* you saw it this time! That was a damn bird in the dining room!

"Hey," you say over the table, "there's a bird in the house!"

■　■　■

That's about the speed of recognition you should expect from your partner regarding your couple money issues. Meaning, if there's a money problem that you're humbly and honestly laying open on the table for discussion with your partner, it may take bringing it up three times (in that humble spirit) before your partner sees the bird.

WHAT IT COSTS TO BE RIGHT

Though we have a responsibility to ourselves and to our partner to have the courage to speak up about our up-to-now unaddressed money problems, we need to avoid the stance of righteousness. If we come to the table acting like a psychologist, we will marginalize our adult partner to the child–parent role. What do kids and teenagers do when their parents act like know-it-alls, without hearing their side? They stuff their feelings or yell back, or they pretend that they agree and then they rebel and do whatever they want. So, you don't want to play parent and you don't want to invest yourself in being right.

Keep this in mind: *What it costs you to be right is your intimacy with others*. I can tell you right now that when we blame our partner and think we have all the answers, we are not being honest with ourselves. The acceptance that we need to work with our partner to solve financial problems is much the same as it is in an addictive cycle: If one partner is debting more than the other, then the less-debting partner is passively consenting—meaning that he or she is an enabling part of the problem.

We're not here to go on a psychological dig into our childhoods, or into our marriages, but we must acknowledge that our need to be right can trigger all kinds of nonsense that is not going to help us get out of debt. In the next few sections of this chapter, I give you some strategies for maintaining a debt-free living partnership, and I also suggest what to do when your partner will not agree to stop debting. For now, though, just put the issue on the table without righteousness, without placing yourself in the know-it-all role.

WE SPEAK OUR TRUTH

So let's say you've reached your limit, or you've "hit bottom," with your couple debt and you're ready to speak up. You understand that (1) you don't have all the answers, (2) you're not innocent, (3) your partner is not solely to blame, and (4) there is a problem and it's a serious one. What do you say exactly? How do you bring it up?

This is how: *You speak the truth, as humbly and honestly as you can.* One of the great tools that the world of popular psychology has given us for better relating to one another is the "I Statement." This is a way of telling our partner (or anyone else) how we're doing or what we're feeling without inventorying the partner's faults. For example, you'd say, "I feel . . ." versus "You did. . . ." Or, "I'm going through a hard time with this . . ." versus "This is what you did to make me act out this way." It is, in fact, not about the other person at all. It's a statement about how *I* am doing. Get it?

"You-did-that-and-it-made-me-do-this" is a dead-end argument. It leads around and around to nowhere. And it leaves each party feeling accused and not heard, attacked and not helped. So, dump that approach at the door. Remember: *You are not going on a psychological excavation of the effects of your past financial history on your relationship.* You know that there is a problem, and that's all you need to know to make a beginning.

SIMPLE AND TRUTHFUL

The statement you make to your partner should be simple. In your own words, you speak your truth. You know there's a serious problem, you don't know how to solve it yet, but you're willing to look at it and create a better way of living. Then you bring it up three times—say, in a two- to three-week time period—and you let your partner have a chance to let it sink in. That's how you begin.

A Debt-Free Spending Plan for Two

Let's say you've read Chapter 3 on creating a Debt-Free Spending Plan, and it all sounds great to you—or like it's worth a try, anyway—but you don't know how to make it work for two people in a serious relationship.

If you query your partnered friends, you will find every permutation of financial management imaginable, right down to the joint-account, no-one-ever-writes-anything-in-the-checkbook approach that so many debting couples are fond of. But often there's one partner who is more responsible for bill paying, or account funding, or both. If there's money trouble, the partner with the purse strings may be likely to hold his or her "parental" role over the head of the other partner. Or the partner who does not pay bills may act out with money, with no accountability. We wish to avoid those scenarios. They do not work to bring peace to a couple's financial life.

Many solvent, financially stable couples succeed with the following scenario: One partner hands over his or her paycheck, and the other is responsible for bill paying and cash allotment. The bill-paying partner is identified as the "better numbers person," the other partner gets some cash to spend—and the couple manages just fine.

But in debtor couples, *both* partners usually have problems dealing not only with debting but also with keeping numbers in general. Both usually are vague about money. So asking one partner to bear the financial-management burden is just asking for trouble. *In debtor couples, no one partner should carry the burden of bill paying; both partners need to be responsible for managing the money.* If one partner is mindlessly spending while the other is sweating bullets figuring out how to pay the bills, then it's an infantilized relationship. The mindless spender gets to be the irresponsible child, and the bill payer gets to be the worried codependent, either afraid to speak up or bellowing at the other with blame and shame. These scenarios will not work in a debt-free life.

So, what do you do if you've been engaging in a less than healthy money scenario? How do you make a new attempt at living debt-free in your relationship? This is what you do: You create a *separate* Debt-Free Spending Plan for each of you, and divide up the Bills. You decide who will pay each Bill each month, you fund your Savings and

Fun Money, and you divide up the cash for living expenses, based on what you have left. You can do this if both of you are working, or if only one partner brings in the income.

The objective is simple: No matter how the Bills are divided up, each partner always has his or her own Spending Plan for Daily Needs, thereby monitoring his or her own spending categories throughout the month.

You essentially create the same spending scenario as presented in Chapters 2 and 3—that is, you assess how much cash income you have each month, and you create a Debt-Free Spending Plan based on those numbers. This time, though, the cash income is going to fund two partners' Spending Plans.

DEBTOR COUPLES NEED TWO CHECKING ACCOUNTS

In a relationship, if both partners have incomes, then it's easy to divide up who pays for each monthly bill based on the cash each brings in. If there's one income, we can still divide up the bills and make each partner responsible for paying half of them—simply by keeping two bank accounts. I recommend this in relationships in which one partner is caring for the home and kids, in school, or is not working outside the home. Why? Because it's important for each partner to develop debt-free living skills and financial responsibility.

When we have two bank accounts, each of us has to be responsible for our part of the joint-living expenses, and each of us can manage the money allotted to us without being micromanaged by our partner. When a couple has been in debt trouble, arguing over each other's debting behavior, the two-account system can be a lifesaver. It takes the dependent, infantilizing blame-game out of the mix.

The powerlessness that results from not having to manage our own money as a partner—no matter how much we long to be "taken care of"—does not serve us as debtors. Our objective is to create responsibility in our independent spending, as well as in our spending as a couple. We can't do that if we're opting out by not participating in the process. Not only that, a parental relationship with our partner in money can de-sexualize the relationship. We are not participating as equals, and we don't feel like equals, and that inequity can affect our accessibility to our partner intimately.

HOW TO BEGIN

Here's how to begin: Sit down with your partner, and list all of your Bills—every last one. It doesn't matter who incurred them; just list them all. Next, take a look at the cash you're bringing in together as a couple, and divide the Bills accordingly, adding them to each partner's individual Debt-Free Spending Plan. Remember: We're only dealing with Bills so far, as in the basic outline for an individual Debt-Free Spending Plan.

If one partner brings in all the cash, the bill paying can be divided by allotting cash to the home-based partner's account and making her or him responsible for paying those bills each month.

It's also fine to pay the bills together from one account, and then divide up the Daily Needs cash and Savings money. But I don't recommend doing that if there's been angst-ridden debt trouble. Why not? Because inevitably, one partner will tend to opt out of the bill-paying process and dump it all on the other partner, claiming, "I'm just no good with numbers!" Asking one person to be responsible for bill paying, in a debtor-couple relationship, is just not fair. When we've been running up debt, it's *hard* to pay our bills, and that pressure should not fall on only one partner's shoulders. Both partners need to step up to the plate and participate for peace to be restored.

In my house, my husband pays the rent, utilities, home phone bill, his health insurance, and car repair expenses. I pay for my own health insurance, both cell phones, both car insurances, my car payment, and renter's insurance. We both fund our separate Savings accounts from our own income, and we keep a joint travel account to use for small or larger trips.

In other words, once we've determined who pays which Bills based on our incomes, we can then craft individual Daily Needs amounts for each of us.

This is where having individual Spending Plans makes the most sense. Remember also that, in the Daily Needs section of our Spending Plans, we're each using a Magic Little Notebook to list our monthly spending amounts, and then we record (and balance) everything we spend. We subtract the amounts we spend as we use money for daily living. It looks like this:

On one page:

Dry Cleaning	30.00
7/10 A-1 Cleaners	−35.00
	−5.00
7/10 From Household	+5.00
	0

And, on another page:

Household	20.00
7/3 Walgreens—kitchen stuff	−7.23
	+12.77
7/10 To Dry Cleaning	−5.00
	+7.77

When each partner has his or her own Spending Plan for food, fuel, dry cleaning, drug store, beauty/personal care, co-pays, household, postage, therapy, and other expenses, then each can use or balance that money however he or she chooses. This means there is no longer any conversation in which one partner shames, controls, or insinuates wrongdoing to the other.

Here's an example. If I choose to skip all dry cleaning one month in favor of hand-washing my blouses, so I can take that cash and buy a new novel, that's my business. If my partner wants to manage food spending so he has an extra $30 to buy coffee drinks or go out to dinner with a friend, that's his business. Our agreement is simple: We always live on cash and we stay out of each other's business. I pay my assigned Bills, he pays his assigned Bills; we fund our Savings, and we live on the rest. How each of us manages our day-to-day cash is none of our partner's business, as long as we're delivering what we agreed to deliver.

MINDING OUR OWN MONEY BUSINESS

In my husband's and my partnership, I put $250 in my Spending Plan for food, buying all of the meat, fish, and produce each month; and I add another $20 for household stuff (things like plastic food wrap and aluminum foil). My partner does all of the Trader Joe's shopping (grocery and a few household items), and allots $300 a month in his Spending Plan for that category. Between the two of us, we cover what we need in grocery and household items with those allotments.

It's none of my business, though, if my husband uses some of his food or household money for something else—like coffee at Peet's or a *New York Times*—as long as he buys what we need. And it's none of his business if I use some of my household money to buy a pair of earrings, or to buy my niece a new lipstick, as long as I can cover my part of what we need for the month. Get it?

Couples with kids should split up the Daily Needs funds to cover what the children need, making each partner responsible for a portion of the kids' spending. For example, Dad might cover the kids' clothing in his Spending Plan because he loves to take his daughters shopping for clothes. Mom might cover medical co-pays, since she's the one who most often takes the kids to the doctor's office. The partners divide up the Daily Needs categories for the kids, allot money to each category, and live within that amount, always living within the family's means.

SEPARATE THE MONEY FOR DAILY NEEDS

Dividing up the bill paying is not absolutely critical for a newly debt-free couple to succeed—though I recommend it—but separating the money for Daily Needs is.

For debtor couples, it's a good idea that money is divided into two accounts and that each partner is responsible for some of the Bills—even if all the cash comes from one income. Do what works for your relationship, acknowledging that each partner needs to have some genuine responsibility in the bill-paying process, but know that you *must* separate the Daily Needs money.

The money for Daily Needs has to be kept separate, for one simple reason: We each need to be given the dignity of managing our own expenses the way we choose to, within the responsible framework we've established in our Debt-Free Spending Plans. *This is where the rubber meets the road in our couple finances.*

When each partner in the relationship has an individual Spending Plan, then we each know what we have to spend on Daily Needs. There's no guessing about what we have to spend in relation to what our partner is spending; there's no overspending while hoping our partner isn't using any cash. We each have a Daily Needs list, and we each list our purchases in our Magic Little Notebook every time we spend money. That way, we both live within our means, and the relationship stays debt-free.

As debtors, we cannot be out in the world without a guide, spending away and trying to balance it all later against what our partner has spent. *There is no way that will work.* That scenario leaves us without a Spending Plan, and that's what has gotten us into debt in the first place. When we spend mindlessly, heads-in-the-sand style, we're purposely being vague so that we can overspend. Vagueness creates drama. And money drama creates nothing but hell in a relationship.

We need to become adults regarding our money, meaning we cannot learn or grow if we have no Spending Plan, or if our partner is managing our every money move, or if we're vaguely spending and hoping our partner isn't using any cash. So, instead we get our own account, our own Debt-Free Spending Plan, and our own Magic Little Notebook—even if it's just to cover a few hundred dollars of Daily Needs expenses each month.

INDIVIDUAL AND JOINT SAVINGS

After funding Bills and Daily Needs, couples can choose to use separate Savings accounts for things that are specific to each partner's needs and dreams, and joint Savings accounts for things that are meaningful to the couple or to family life. For instance, a couple may put $40 toward a new Sport Bike Savings account for him, $40 toward an Outlet Shopping Savings account for her, while funding $240 for a joint College Savings account for the kids. There are infinite variations, so make it work for the two of you. In any event, be fair. Be reasonable. And tell the truth about what you really, really want to save some money for, even if it seems like you're putting away a small amount.

Remember that it's *beginning* to save for what's meaningful to us that creates a shift in our ability to creatively fund what we love. We don't lie about what we really want just because we're in a committed relationship. We just begin, even if that beginning is humble. To fund what we love, especially in a relationship, helps each of us feel that we are our true selves in the partnership. And that can only create more intimacy and more peace for us.

Victoria and Mark's Spending Plans

In developing our individual Spending Plans, we note that each partner needs different things. Each has different priorities, different needs, and different outcomes to achieve. The following is an example of how to craft a Debt-Free Spending Plan for two in a relationship. Note how Victoria and Mark have divided up their Bills category, and how each has different priorities reflected in his or her Daily Needs.

VICTORIA AND MARK'S SPENDING PLANS

Mark's Monthly Spending Plan (July)

Income

July 1st paycheck	$4,082.00
Total	$4,082.00

Necessities

Bills	$2,338.76
Daily Needs	749.00
Total	$3,087.76

Balance

$4,082.00 (income) − 3,087.76 (expenses) = $994.24

Savings, Vacation, and Fun	**$994.24**
Fun & Entertainment Money	300.00
Healthy Reserve (joint)	120.00
Short-Term Savings Account (joint)	140.00
Car Repair Savings	98.00
New Computer Savings	50.00
Retirement Savings	142.24
Travel Account (joint)	144.00
Total	994.24

Monthly Plan Detail

Bills	**Due**	**Amount**
Rent	1st	1,594.00
Health Insurance	1st	comes out of check
Long-Term Health Care	3rd	68.76
Rx (monthly)	1st	86.00
Car	[paid off!]	
PG&E	23rd	18.00
Phone, home	18th	91.00
Netflix	1st	11.00
Moveable Feast	1st	30.00
Gym	10th	65.00 auto deduction
Visa (debt repayment)	3rd	350.00
Casual Dining	1st	25.00
Total		2,338.76

Daily Needs	Amount
Food	302.00
Coffee	25.00
Lunches	20.00
Fuel/Park	235.00
Co-pays	20.00
Drug Store	30.00
Dry Cleaners	20.00
Laundry Home (coin ops)	21.00
Household	11.00
Postage	5.00
Clothing	60.00
Total	749.00

Mark earns more than Victoria and has fewer Daily Needs in his category. The couple chose to spend more of his income on savings for things like travel for the two of them and a new computer. Since Mark's debting downfall was dining out on credit, the couple agreed to put $300 per month of his income aside to cover Fun Money and dining out for the two of them. Mark also adds another $25 for casual dining—a stash they put in an envelope for an end-of-the-month cheap meal. The couple has agreed to dine at reasonably priced locales, so $300 can cover dining, movie, and general entertainment costs for a month with little trouble.

Mark has one major debt that he brought into the relationship, which he pays at the rate of $350 per month—$40 over his minimum.

Victoria's Monthly Spending Plan (July)

Income	
July 6 paycheck	$1,445.00
July 20 paycheck	1,445.00
Total	$2,890.00
Necessities	
Bills	$1,345.10
Daily Needs	1,009.00
Total	$2,354.10

Balance

$2,890.00 (income) − 2,354.10 (expenses) = $535.90

Savings, Vacation, and Fun	**$535.90**
Fun Money	100.00
Healthy Reserve (joint)	100.00
Short-Term Savings Account (joint)	120.00
Electric Car Savings Account	115.90
Travel Account (joint)	100.00
Total	535.90

Monthly Plan Detail

Bills	Due	Amount
Car Payment	28th	394.00
Cell for both	21st	165.00
Health Insurance	1st	460.00
Car Insurance for both	10th	116.32
Gym	7th	49.00
Renter's insurance	15th	23.78
Automatic Savings	10th	25.00
Credit Card—Visa	27th	45.00 min
Credit Card—Chase	25th	67.00 min
Total		1,345.10

Daily Needs	Amount
Food (Groceries)	250.00
Fuel	225.00
Parking/Tolls/Public Transit	10.00
Medical Co-Pays	30.00
Drug Store	20.00
Beauty/Personal Care	25.00
Clothing	80.00
Dry Cleaning	30.00
Laundry Home (coin-ops)	20.00
Household	20.00
Postage	9.00
Haircut (envelope, every three months)	40.00

Entertainment	20.00
Tennis lessons	70.00
Acupuncture	150.00
Cash Contributions	10.00
Total	1,009.00

Note that Victoria has a car payment and pays for her own health insurance—Bills that Mark does not have, and both are factored into their agreement about which partner will pay which Bills. Victoria makes less money, so the couple agreed that Mark will cover the rent, and then they split the other Bills between them, so that all Bills are covered. Victoria also has more Daily Needs in that she plays tennis—a stress reliever for her that both partners agree significantly enhances their marriage. She also has a physical problem that only acupuncture has helped to relieve, so those expenses are represented in her Spending Plan.

Note also that there are additions that work for both partners. Mark adds "Moveable Feast" to his Bills—an account that he and several friends fund each month, and then every few years they fund a trip for themselves from it. Victoria's Bills are straightforward and clear, but she has more Daily Needs to cover, including a beauty category and higher clothing costs for her job—expenses that her husband doesn't have.

All of these expenses are realistically factored into the couple's decisions about how to spend the cash they have. Neither is asked to go without money for realistic needs. "Realistic needs" are things that are required or asked of us in daily life. A man or woman who is working downtown might need lunch money or snack money. Most women are going to need makeup money—an expense a male partner won't (usually) have. Women's clothes are going to be more expensive, simply because it takes more varieties of clothing to be appropriate in various social and work circumstances. Each partner will need some recreation money—Fun Money that's theirs and only theirs. When times are tight, chrome on the Harley is not a necessity. When times are tight, $175 facials are not a necessity. So, we don't argue over allocating cash. We're realistic, honest, and, for now, we're frugal.

Nobody Wants to Be Told What to Do

The last piece of the couple's "money puzzle" is simply a psychological one. In a partnership, we *hate* to be told what to do. We want to be respected as adults, to be treated like grown-ups, and to be spoken to from a place of equality and dignity. That said, neither of us has been respectful of our relationship if we're in debt. We've caused each other stress, anxiety, worry, doubt, and fear by debting, and we've both watched the train veer off the tracks, avoiding and dodging the issue. We have added to a feeling of being trapped in our relationship financially, and that has hindered our ability to respect and be intimate with our partner.

So, though we each deserve the dignity of having our own Spending Plan (and not having our partner micromanage our spending), we need to take on that new responsibility with genuine humility. Once again, our amends will be made in our changed behavior. We will prove ourselves by following our Spending Plan, by being responsible for our individual spending inside our relationship, and by being able to make money decisions and money adjustments within our partnership without drama.

In other words, *we do not get to go over our monthly amounts and then ask our partner to bail us out.* We are responsible for what we have to spend, and we live within our means. That's what will bring respect, peace, and sanity back to our partnership.

The Aphrodisiac Quality of a Debt-Free Spending Plan

The very best and unsuspecting outcome of a Debt-Free Spending Plan for Two is that it is an absolutely exquisite aphrodisiac. You'll think I'm joking, but I'm truly not. Mutual Debt-Free Spending Plans will, I guarantee you, change the way you and your partner feel about each other—and that, in turn, will affect your ability to be intimate with each other.

Once the money tension leaves our couple's life, it also leaves our bedroom. Peace is restored, and sanity begins to enter our daily life again. Intimacy is restored because we are not harboring low-level angst, resentment, or anger. We feel that our partner has become more accessible to us. We both feel better about ourselves and about each other. We feel like responsible adults. And though it doesn't seem like being responsible would automatically result in more intimacy, somehow it does. We feel better in our partner's presence—both publicly and privately.

A PERSONAL SUCCESS STORY

I became extremely proud of my husband—and of us both as a couple—when we began to use our Spending Plans to live debt-free. Suddenly, we were talking openly about our money challenges, and our willingness *to do something about them as a couple* meant we were no longer stuck. I felt delighted with our progress, even when it was imperfect. I became happier with him and happier with our life together, in simple, daily ways. The stress went out of our conversations, our daily encounters, and our bedroom.

Think about it. When we are not adding to our debting balances, when we do not have our heads in the sand, ignoring the mounting debts, and when we are no longer blaming each other for our money failures, we find that we *like* each other more. We're no longer acting out of unresolved anger or unaddressed problems. We no longer feel as if our financial challenges have trapped us in a corner with our partner. Or course, we will still have money decisions, but we won't have money drama. And no matter how simply we're living, our days will feel better together, without the added stress of mounting debt.

Without that elephant in the hallway, blocking our paths to each other, it's a very sweet swoon into the bedroom.

Lawyers, Guns, and Money

So what happens when one partner wants to live debt-free and the other flatly refuses? If we've had enough of our disastrous couple finances and we can't take it anymore, and our partner is unwilling to be part of living debt-free, does that mean we have to bring in the big guns and file for divorce? Does it mean that our marriage is absolutely over? No, it doesn't. There are still ways we can help ourselves—ways to live debt-free even though our partner chooses not to. We cannot control another person's behavior. We can make choices about what we will do and where we will place ourselves in relation to others, including our partner.

So how do we negotiate this delicate territory? First, we sit down, solo, and list all of the Bills we have—meaning, we review all of the monthly amounts. Then, with our best shot at fairness, we plot out what we're willing to pay for each month. Then, we craft a Debt-Free Spending Plan for ourselves, including our allotted Bills, Daily Needs, Savings, and Fun Money. We then share it with our partner, and let him or her know exactly what we will be paying for each month. We do not pay one dime more than we agreed to pay.

In other words, if I'm agreeing to pay for the meat, fish and produce, and my partner's supposed to get the juice, milk, bread, cereal, and paper towels, and he gouges his income in some way and doesn't come through, then there's no paper towels or juice this month. We do not bail out a debting partner! We let the partner experience the outcomes of his or her own actions. And we never, ever, go into debt ourselves to cover a partner's losses.

So what do you do if the refusing partner is the one who brings in all the income and handles all the bills? You ask, first, to split up the Bills—to be made responsible for paying half of them. You ask for cash to cover your part of the Bills and your Daily Needs, and you get your own checking account. You pay for the critical things like food, fuel, and your own expenses. Each month, you receive your amounts from your partner for the necessities you need to cover, you put the money in your account, and you live within that amount. You let your partner know you will not be debting for anything, anymore.

SAY NO TO DEBTING "PRESENTS"

Here's where it gets interesting. If your partner is still debting, what do you do when he or she goes into debt to buy something for you? What if your partner says, "Hey, let's go out tonight—it's on me," and you know that a credit card will be used to pay for it? *We absolutely have to refuse gifts that are given to us by a debting partner.* We cannot, in good conscience, pretend that we're doing our part by balancing our own money, while allowing our partner to dig a deeper hole by debting for couple gifts, luxuries, or expenses.

What this means—let me spell it out—is that you cannot agree to go on trips, go out to dinner, accept gifts, or receive expense items that are paid for with credit cards from your partner. *Since we cannot control another person's behavior, how on God's green earth do we manage that?* Just do the best you can to set a boundary. You know the state of your couple finances, so you can usually guess what's being paid for by credit—or you witness it, when the credit card is laid down on top of the dinner check.

If you're at all self-righteous or controlling about your stance, you can start a holy war with your partner over this boundary, so your objective is to not be righteous. Your goal is to say, clearly and calmly, "I'm not using credit or debting anymore, so I can't in good conscience go out to dinner with you on credit." That's all. No drama. No whining. No allowing yourself to be "convinced" into letting your partner debt for you. You just set your boundary and stick to it.

Early in my relationship with my husband, I was miserable in my work, going from high-stress job to high-stress job. Instead of dealing with the issue as a couple, we would go out to dinner to stave off the angst. My husband would debt to take me out, and that would shut me up for a while—long enough to bury the issue a little longer. He was afraid of my leaning on him financially—specifically, he feared what would happen if I stopped earning, or earned less while I figured out what I could do for work—and I was afraid to bring home less money because he expected a certain lifestyle from me. To earn less would also have meant facing our debting lifestyle, and neither of us was prepared to do that. But the debting just dug us a bigger hole, made me feel more trapped in a job I hated, and I grew to resent him, myself, and our marriage. The pressure weighed us both down, and the additional debting made us feel poor and desperate. It was not a scenario that led to anything good.

You want to stay out of those death-trap partnership scenarios as much as possible. Instead, you want to do your part to face your financial challenges, and take steps to correct your part of the couple-money dysfunction. When you stop accepting debtor gifts from your partner and you do your part to live within your means, you leap, truly, into a new kind of living—a way of life that will bring peace and ease to your partnership and to your individual life.

SEPARATE CREDIT LINES ARE CRITICAL

If your partner is still running up balances and you've stopped, what do you do about joint credit lines? Simple: You separate everything. You cancel all joint cards. If you own a house, you *make sure*—no guessing—that two signatures are required for any credit loaned against house equity. If you have an open credit line against the house, change it or close it in favor of a two-signature requirement (meaning, again, that one of you can't draw cash against home equity without the other's signature). Since you're not going to debt against yourself by using your home equity to live on, you won't be signing any loan that uses it.

What I recommend, if you have a still-debting partner, is to keep no joint credit cards or credit lines. Once you have agreed with yourself to live debt-free, then you cut up (and call to cancel) all of your own cards and accounts, anyway; that means credit cards, credit lines, technology and department store cards—all of them. By closing all joint accounts as well, you put a cap on all your couple credit spending and you can then address the debt repayment without adding more to the balances. You cannot stop your partner from opening a new, individual credit card account, but you can take your name off all joint accounts by closing them and capping the debt.

It helps, after that, to create a document that states that each partner's debt is his or her own. You may think that this action is over the top—that it's not necessary or that your partner's debt is no big deal if you've stopped debting. But with debtors, it is always a big deal. Debtors are compulsive, and we spend in addictive cycles. And if we want to live debt-free but our partner does not, a written agreement is a way of making ourselves very clear. (You can get the agreement notarized, which, according to one Los Angeles–based family-law attorney, will protect you from your partner's individual debts should the marriage dissolve.) As before, you approach this agreement with humility and courage—no yelling or demanding.

Hope, Backed by Action

When you use the Debt-Free Spending Plan and the tips offered in this chapter, you are taking a powerful stand for peace, ease, and loving behavior in your relationship. You bring hope to your partnership instead of fear. You bring an ability to work together to solve problems instead of ignoring the problems and waiting for the situation to blow up. You risk speaking the truth, humbly and honestly, so that your relationship can be free of money stress.

The power of hope in love can sweep the entire relationship landscape like a strong wind blowing a thunderstorm out of a dark valley. But hope by itself is not enough. We have to back it up with action. If all we're willing to do is state the need for change, but we're not willing to back it up with concrete steps to change our behavior, we will end up creating more hopelessness in our relationships. Distrust will grow between us as partners, and it will taint all of our interactions.

The good news is that we don't have to create the action steps by ourselves. The Debt-Free Spending Plan is here to help. When we use the Spending Plan to learn to live debt-free together, we have a powerful tool for creating harmony in our love relationships—in both our money decisions and our ability to communicate about them. Peace will replace stress. Trust will replace blame. And as any couple who has stopped fighting about money and debt can tell you, those changes are worth their weight in gold.

8

. . . . .

"Mom, Can I Borrow. . .?"

How to Stop Asking for Money and Start Paying It Back

THE MOST COMMON thing I encounter in my Debt-Free Living coaching is unpaid family and personal loans. It's as if, for debtors, our most intimate loans are invisible to us. When we're in money trouble, we often first stop paying back the loans given us by our parents, our siblings, or our friends. We figure they'll "understand." My guess is that because there is no credit collector at the other end of these private loans, and often no interest, we feel we can skate on them "until things get better." The trouble with that argument is that because we're debtors, there never is a better time to pay, only a deepening cycle of debt.

We debtors live in a world of mental justifications regarding personal loans. "Well, it's my mom and dad; they have to love me," or "It's just going to come out of my inheritance anyway," or "They really owe me, since I put myself through college." So let's clear this up right now: *If you made an agreement to accept a loan, then you have a responsibility to pay it back on a regular, monthly basis.*

There is no justification for not repaying a loan we accepted from a family member or a friend. As much as we'd like to rationalize our nonpayments, spinning excuses in our heads, we need to face the facts: If we are not paying, then we are out of integrity with the person who gave us cash. All of that hype about how our money loaner should understand that our finances are poor, and shouldn't expect us to pay back our loan, is really just rubbish. You know it and I know it. *We strain and ruin relationships by not paying back the money we owe.*

And, just like when we addressed our past debting history, we're not going to go on an archeological dig into how we've treated the people in our lives with regard to money we owe; we're just going to correct what we've done wrong. We admit that it is wrong, and that we need to change that, and we focus on the change. We create a strategy—starting today—to amend that situation.

How Much Do You Owe?

Many of us who have borrowed from friends or family "don't remember" what we owe—which could certainly be looked at as a comfortable bit of denial—not wanting to face how much we've borrowed. If we fall into this category, we do not need to despair. We will simply do the best we can to reconcile what we suspect we owe. We will write down everything we can remember, and then we'll take at least a week or two to ruminate on it, noting any forgotten amounts that come back to us.

And, along with that, we will go to whatever lengths we need to find out what we owe. If that means we have to contact the county for records of loans taken against our brother's or our father's house, then we do it. If that means talking to our controlling sister who's our mother's executor, we call and ask how much we owe, as humbly as possible. We do not lowball the amounts, or try to get out of amounts we owe by arguing. We just get clarity as best we can on what we owe and we begin to pay it back, a little at a time.

Our apology for nonpayment is made in our changed behavior. It's not enough to say "I'm sorry" and continue with the same non-payment and debt-dismissive attitude. We're not only learning to live debt-free; we're also beginning to live with integrity regarding our money. And no matter how challenging that looks right now, in no time at all we're going to feel better—about our money, our financial picture, and ourselves.

One woman I know had borrowed from her mother year after year, and had not kept track of the amounts she borrowed. When she made a "money apology" to her mom, she admitted that she didn't know what she owed. She was shocked to find out that her mom had kept a list in a small notebook in a drawer—covering eight years of loans—and gave the amount off the top of her head. In other words, just because we're not keeping track of the amounts doesn't mean the person who loaned us money isn't keeping track. So we make it right to the best of our ability.

You Pay What You Can

Does paying back personal loans mean we have to struggle, scrape, and deprive ourselves to pay back the $80,000 we borrowed from our folks? No, it does not. We employ the same principles we applied to our credit card and loan payments. We allot a reasonable minimum, and we begin to repay. The difference here is that family members or friends are not banks; they will not set a minimum payment for us. *We have to do it.* So we set a reasonable amount, in relation to our own Spending Plan, and we pay it, every month.

We don't worry if the monthly amount is small. Intention works miracles in money. If we owe $80,000 and we can reasonably pay back $50 a month to our folks, then so be it. If we can reasonably pay more, then we do. We don't lowball our debt repayment, nor do we gouge our living expenses. We make it work within our Spending Plan, so that our repayments are not making us unable to meet our needs.

We are working the same principles here that have been promoted earlier in this book: (1) we let our Debt-Free Spending Plan help us structure the amounts for living expenses that are reasonable; (2) we create Savings and Fun Money categories, setting aside the cash that makes for a good life; and (3) we repay debts in amounts that are reasonable and balanced in relation to our living expenses.

How to Make Money Amends

So what do we do if our relationships are strained with those family members or friends who loaned us money? And how do we determine if there is an issue about our nonpayment if everything seems fine on the surface?

Here's how. We *assume*, at the very least, that our nonpayment has caused a loss of trust between us and our money loaners, and that we are viewed as less than responsible and less than reliable. That means that we owe those people an apology. We need to make amends. (I believe this is true for creditors, too, because at the end of the day, our credit card companies are made up of people who once had faith in us. Sure, credit card companies encourage debt to make a profit, but we made a promise to pay back the money we borrowed. That's what we're dealing with here.)

So, how do we proceed to make an apology to the person we have not paid? We say something simple, to the point, and clear. Our apology can be something like this:

Sis, I wanted to talk to you about the money I owe you. I'm working hard on a Spending Plan to live debt-free, and as part of that, I'm paying back money I owe, even if it's just a small amount. I'm going to start paying you $50 on the first of the month toward the loan you gave me. I'm sorry that it's taken me so long, and I'm sorry for any lack of trust you have in me for not paying. I'm changing that, and I thank you for your understanding.

A few sentences is all you need. No long diatribes, no emotional outpourings—keep it short and sweet. If your relationship with your money loaner is fraught with tension, then write your apology on a nice note card and send it with your first check. Know that your efforts will be worthless if you apologize and don't back it up with action. In fact, it will cause a deeper lack of trust—just like an alcoholic who swears she'll never drink again and shows up drunk the next week. So, make your genuine apology by changing your behavior—meaning that you pay back your debt, a little at a time. Do it on time, every month, and watch your relationships change for the better.

REGAIN THE RESPECT OF THOSE WHO LOVE YOU

Many of us debtors are so embarrassed about our money issues and our nonpayment of family and friend loans that we'd rather ignore the issue than pay some "measly" amount, like $50 against an $80,000 loan. Know this: *You will not get better until you have financial integrity with all of your expenses— including your personal debts.*

Most people, when faced with our sincere willingness to change, will offer their understanding and will appreciate our effort. As in all things debt-free, we begin small, and the consciousness of our actions breeds an ability over time to fund or pay back more than we ever thought we could. We just begin. We do the right thing, and we leave the discussion of amounts alone.

Loans, Gifts, and Debt Forgiveness

Sometimes we debtors like to kid ourselves about personal loans, justifying or manipulating them into "gifts." Here's the difference between a loan and a gift: The terms of a loan include paying money back; the terms of a gift do not. It's that simple.

To answer the question, "Was this a loan or a gift?" we simply ask ourselves: *Did I say I would pay it back?* If the answer is yes, then we don't angle for turning a loan into a gift after the fact. That's just manipulation.

Sometimes parents who have cash to give will say, "Never mind about the loan; we'll just make it a gift since you're struggling." Should we insist on paying it back? That depends upon the relationship. There is nothing wrong with debt forgiveness, as long as our behavior has actually changed. If we accept debt forgiveness, and then we keep debting and borrowing from our parents, we're just like the alcoholic who keeps promising to stop drinking and keeps going on benders.

Here's a general rule of thumb: If you offer to pay back your loan, and make your amends, and the person still says, "I want to forgive this loan to help you live debt-free," then take some time to consider the effects that may have on your friendship or family relationship. If you can truly say that you have changed your behavior, that you have stopped debting and are living debt-free, *and all your credit lines and cards are cut up with the accounts closed*, then you can accept the debt forgiveness.

Warning: Don't share your use of the Debt-Free Spending Plan as a ploy to angle for debt forgiveness if you're still running up your credit lines. If you're not ready to stop debting or borrowing, then you're not ready to change. But you don't want to dig a *deeper* hole for yourself by using the helping tools in this book to fake out your lenders so you can borrow more cash.

Most parents or friends who've loaned cash will signal that they expect repayment by accepting the terms of your money amends. They'll say, "Thank you for making that effort; I've been waiting for you to acknowledge the loan," or "I appreciate that you're starting to pay me back." That means you are on target; your amends and your repayment have hit at the heart of the relationship issue between you and your loaner. You repay with humility and thankfulness, grateful for the opportunity to repair the damage done.

One of my clients, Terry-Ann, told her parents that she had created a Debt-Free Spending Plan and also that she had significant debt to the IRS. After a few weeks, her parents called her and offered to pay off her IRS debt. Since Terry-Ann had been living debt-free for two years, she had the integrity to accept the offer, but she didn't feel great about doing so. Her parents had often used her inability to handle her finances as a way to shame her, and she didn't want more of that, especially after all her terrific efforts to live debt-free.

After thinking it through, she agreed to allow them to pay $9,500 of her $19,000 IRS debt, and then she leveraged that amount against her inheritance (i.e., she will get $9,500 less than her sisters in her parents' will). After paying half the amount due the IRS, she was then able to negotiate her debt down by several thousand dollars, and in a little over a year she had paid off the balance.

Here's the bottom line on debt forgiveness or debt-payoff gifts: If the offer is made, we don't accept unless our behavior has changed and we are truly living debt-free. If it's not offered, we do not angle for it or manipulate the situation to get it. We are responsible for our own debt repayment, we use our Spending Plan to address it, and we live debt-free. That's it in a nutshell.

The One-Third Windfall Money Rule

Sometimes family members will offer genuine gifts of cash. Parents may offer end-of-year cash gifts or friends may say, "Here, I've got a bunch of cash this year. Here's a check." Whenever there's a cash offer from family or friends, we always say, "Respectfully, I need to know if this is a gift or a loan. I don't debt anymore so clarity is important to me."

Once we know it is a gift, we accept (or not) graciously, and we apply the One-Third Windfall Money Rule. That is, one-third of the amount goes to debt repayment, one-third goes to Savings accounts, and one-third goes to Fun Money or anything else we choose. If our income is unstable and we need living-expense money, then that's what we use the gift for, in whole or in part, depending on our delineated Spending Plan needs.

For example, one of my clients was working very hard to live debt-free, and she had paid back or negotiated down over $60,000 in debt over three years, while living on a lower than normal salary. She then lost her job. Since she had a Healthy Reserve and money in Savings, she was not desperate, but when her parents offered her a gift of $2,500, she hesitated. She asked me, should she accept? We agreed that *a gift is a gift*. She decided she would receive the gift graciously, knowing that she was living debt-free, and her parents felt good about giving the money, knowing that they were contributing to her new way of life and her job search.

9

. . . . .

Creativity, Not
Credit Cards

Learning from the Spending
Plans of the Newly Debt-Free

IF YOU HAVE read this far in this book, you've learned a lot.
You've learned the structure of the Debt-Free Spending Plan, how
it works, and the simple steps it will take to create your own
Spending Plan. You've learned how to create meaningful savings,
how to cut expenses to live within your means, and how to create a
Debt-Repayment Plan that doesn't gouge your living expenses.
You've also explored couples' strategies and debt repayment for personal loans. You've learned that though there are certainly issues that
have caused you to get into debt, they won't stand in your way of living debt-free, *as long as you use the tools offered in this book.*

This chapter helps you to *practice* using the tools by showing you real examples of Spending Plans in action. These examples will help you get familiar with the details that will impact your own Debt-Free Spending Plan. So, let's review the steps needed to begin creating your own debt-free life:

1. Agree to stop debting and freeze, cut up, and/or cancel all credit lines and credit cards.

2. Create a personal Debt-Free Spending Plan and begin to live within it.

3. Use Savings accounts and Fun Money to fund what you love, even if you're saving small amounts.

4. Develop a Debt-Repayment Plan that addresses what you can reasonably pay, no matter how low, and still fund all your needs.

When I began working my own Debt-Free Spending Plan, I made changes in both my Bills and my Daily Needs spending that required both my humility and my behavioral willingness. I stopped shopping at high-end grocery stores and I started buying from local produce markets and ethnic groceries. I got a cheaper cell phone plan and better-priced car insurance. I stopped buying any expensive cosmetics and bought $2 and $4 lipsticks from the drugstore instead.

I bought facial creams from an online health food store. I stopped using all high-end shampoos and hair products, and bought "natural" products online. I found a cheaper—and better—hair stylist. I washed my own car. I used the Student Acupuncture Clinic. I got massages at an off-the-beaten-track spot that had a regular, half-price special. I stopped with the high-end waxing and started going to a small, clean, no-frills salon that charges $24 for a bikini wax. I started machine- and hand-washing more of my clothes. I cleaned my own house. I changed where I bought household items, where I got my shoes repaired, and who altered my clothing.

I got my needs met, but I got them met *cheaper*. And, you know what? My lifestyle didn't really change. What changed was that I had money for vacations, dining, clothing, savings, and fun that didn't ask me to incur one dime of debt. What I got out of these changes, this living-by-the-bottom-line, was peace with my money. And the process of doing it didn't run my life. Amazing.

Downsizing Means Things Are Looking Up

As we get ready to look at some real-world Debt-Free Spending Plans, it can be easy to suffer some shell-shocked depression about having to stop spending more than we earn. This means, in most cases, that we're going to spend less. So, this is a good moment to take a breath, and let the following thought sink into our minds and hearts: *We, as yet, have no idea how much better it is going to feel to buy with no debt, even if we're buying less.*

We've been spending more than we earn because we believe we need to, and we're terrified that if we spend less, we won't have enough. But the Debt-Free Spending Plan is here to help us make sure we do have enough. "Enough," though, is going to look and feel different from here on out.

Beyond our I-really-don't-want-to-deal-with-my-debting-issues-but-I-know-that-I-have-to attitude, there is a place of ease where we learn to spend well and spend debt-free. We already know that we have been guiltily running up debt and hoarding stuff—food, clothes, entertainment, sporting gear—you name it. But what we don't know yet is what's ahead. It's something we've never experienced before. That is, to feel peace with every single purchase we make.

So, as you review the numbers in each example Spending Plan that follows in this chapter, recognize that you can live on less than you're spending now, that you can live debt-free, and that, though the numbers may seem so very different from what you expect you need, you can live simply, peacefully, and solvent—and still get all of your needs met.

"NO" IS A COMPLETE SENTENCE

Remember that you're going to evaluate what's worth spending money on and what's not. You are the one setting up your personal Debt-Free Spending Plan. And if your income won't allow you to spend what you've been spending and live free from debt, then you have to choose what the "keepers" and the "cuts" are. The only rule here is that it's all got to come out balanced at your bottom line. What you keep and what you cut is up to you.

That said, once you're using your Spending Plan, you might find yourself unable to say no when you need to for unexpected money demands—a hangover, for sure, from your debting days. But you're going to need this skill to make your real-world Debt-Free Spending Plan work for you. The inability to say no to unexpected money demands is one of the core problems that triggered our debt crisis in the first place. *We don't want to admit that we can't afford things.* Playing at being richer than we are has gotten us into sad and sorry shape, both financially and emotionally. So we need to learn to use the word no, and we need to learn that skill now.

Here's an example. Allison found that her consulting work continually made her feel pressured to dine out, meeting potential clients for lunch—which, in the first month of her Spending Plan, gouged her dining and grocery categories significantly. The kicker was that she didn't really want to go on these lunches and would much rather have had more clothing money, a more flush grocery category, and some extra dining-out money that was social, not business related. These lunches also ended up taking a huge bite of time out of her work day (usually three hours), which impacted her work output.

She also caught herself not being able to say no to expensive family birthday gifts and to regular $30 breakfasts with friends that she also really didn't want to go to. Her downsized Spending Plan didn't allow her to raid her food, fuel, or other categories for these events and still have enough to live well all month long, and her dining category wasn't enough to cover these expenses and still have something left for herself.

So, Allison and I worked on coming up with some simple language that would communicate her priorities without embarrassment: "Lunches aren't good for me this week—but I can meet you for coffee at three." Or, "Breakfast won't work for me—but I can go for a hike at ten." With group dinners, which always ended up being overly costly with wealthier or overspending friends, she said, "I'd be happy to make pasta at my place, but dinner out isn't on my dance card this month." In other words, saying no means you have to tell the truth! You let the people in your inner circle know that you're working a Debt-Free Spending Plan; and in the business world, where you may not want to reveal your money challenges, you set clear and clean boundaries. You say no when you mean it.

After just a month of practicing saying no, Allison felt a weight lifted off her shoulders. She got more done during the day, she limited her time with potential clients until they became paying clients, and she had more money for socializing and dining for fun. Now, she meets all of her new clients for coffee or in their offices, limiting her time spent, as well as limiting her expenses—and she keeps more cash for herself.

DEBT, DAILY NEEDS, AND "BALLPARKING"

As I noted in Chapter 3, Daily Needs are the arena we've been most afraid to "budget" or limit ourselves, for fear that our needs won't get met. It's also likely that these are the categories in which we have the least amount of accountability, spending blindly with no plan.

So, as we review the Debt-Free Spending Plans in this chapter, remember that, after listing our Bills, we will *ballpark* what we think we really need—monthly—to cover our Daily Needs. That means we have to come up with numbers for food, fuel, clothing, personal care, and several other things. To do that, we use the simple categories outlined in Chapter 2, and we adjust as needed.

Why are we ballparking at first? Because we probably don't have clear historical totals of how much we spend in each Daily Needs area per month. Even if we do, our totals probably vary wildly on everything from food to household items, because without a Spending Plan, we have had no guidelines for what we can or should spend each month. Our totals from past months will give us *some* idea of what we've been spending, but they won't tell us what we can *afford* to spend. Since we're not going to do a financial analysis of our past spending habits, we'll have to guess at first, and then be flexible, adjusting as we go.

It will take about three months of using the Debt-Free Spending Plan—adjusting and tweaking it—to get a reasonable handle on what it really costs you to live each month. I'm mentioning this again to address the perfectionist in each of us who wants to find *salvation* in the first week of working the Debt-Free Spending Plan. We'll get there. For now, just do your best.

Five Real-World Examples

The objective of the Debt-Free Spending Plan is to have one central place in which we list everything we will need and everything we will spend in one month, in a simple summary. Yes, things will fluctuate a little, and we'll adapt to those fluctuations. Things will come up that we didn't plan for, and we'll adjust our Spending Plan to deal with those things. But what we're *not* going to do anymore is put money into our bank accounts and just wing it, paying a bunch of Bills and spending a bunch of cash with no clarity, so that we never have any money afterward for the things that are meaningful to us.

So, let's take a look at some typical Spending Plans. Reviewing real-world Spending Plans will help you get used to the Spending Plan's tools, and will offer you practice that will come in handy when you set up your own Spending Plan. I've included real plans from real clients. They are used with each client's permission, though the names have been changed. These real-life Spending Plans will give you a more complete sense of what a Spending Plan looks like, and how it can be adjusted for your specific needs.

Simply stated, the more you practice using the Spending Plan, the easier it will become for you. If you don't see your spending levels covered in the first or second examples, please don't tune out. I've purposely chosen some simple examples and some more complex ones, representing average, mid-range, and middle-to-upper incomes for both full- and part-time workers. Your income may be higher or lower than the examples, but the principles are the same, so use these Spending Plans as models, even if your numbers don't match up exactly.

Alanna's Debt-Free Spending Plan

Here is Alanna's first-pass Debt-Free Spending Plan, followed by detailed notes. Alanna earns exactly $60,000 each year at her office job. She has more than $45,000 in credit card debt—mostly from clothing purchases, dining out, and trips she's paid for with credit. Her first-pass Spending Plan did not balance, which is the case with most of our first-round attempts. But on her second try, she was able to create a debt-free version that she could live with. Note that Alanna had been spending almost double what she's making, and she was still able to make changes that created a workable Debt-Free Spending Plan.

ALANNA'S FIRST-PASS SPENDING PLAN (JULY)

Income	
July 4 paycheck	$1,447.32
July 18 paycheck	1,447.32
Health Insurance Reimbursement	349.00
Total	$3,243.64

Necessities	
Bills	$2,880.88

Daily Needs	2,610.00
Total	$5,490.88

Balance

$3,243.64 (income)−5,490.88 (expenses) = $−2,247.24

Note that Alanna's ballparked expenses are almost double what she's bringing in each month, which accounts for the upturn in her debt balances in the past two years.

Savings, Vacation, and Fun Money	**0.00**
Fun Money	0.00
Healthy Reserve	0.00
Short-Term Savings	0.00
Travel Fund	0.00
New Wardrobe Account	0.00
Three Months in South America	0.00
Total	0.00

Since Alanna is negative in her monthly spending, she can't fund any of the priority areas she identified as personal wants and savings needs.

Monthly Plan Detail

Bills	**Due**	**Amount**
Rent (includes utilities)	1st	1,145.00
Renter's Insurance	8th	45.00
Health Insurance	7th	325.00
Car Payment	5th	294.00
Cell Phone	15th	88.00
Car Insurance	10th	119.22 auto deduct
Yoga Studio	1st	145.00
Cable	3rd	117.55
Visa	10th	254.00 min
MasterCard	5th	108.11 min
Kohl's	17th	54.00 min
JCrew	12th	49.00 min

Victoria's Secret	7th	88.00 min
Nordstrom	15th	49.00 min
Total		2,880.88

Daily Needs	Amount
Food (Groceries)	300.00
Fuel	225.00
Parking/Tolls/Public Transit	10.00
Medical Co-Pays	30.00
Drug Store	35.00
Beauty/Personal Care	55.00
Clothing	200.00
Dry Cleaning	100.00
Household	50.00
Postage	10.00
Haircut	225.00
Entertainment	20.00
Plane Flights	450.00
Dining	450.00
Massage Therapy	250.00
Nail Salon	200.00
Total	2,610.00

By reviewing Alanna's Bills and Daily Needs, we can see very quickly where her trouble areas are. Those same trouble areas will help us determine what she needs to fund—in terms of Daily Needs—so she doesn't continue to debt.

REVIEWING ALANNA'S FIRST-PASS PLAN

Alanna was living well beyond her means, racking up $2,247.24 in new debt each month—a rate of increase that would quickly run up more debt than her annual income. When we talked about it, Alanna admitted that the more she saw her balances go up, the more reckless she felt about adding to them. Her feeling was, "I'm never going to be able to pay these credit lines off, so what difference does it make if I add to them?" Many of us who have experienced spiraling debt have felt and acted the same way.

When we took a closer look at her Spending Plan, Alanna was able to see that her needs were not necessarily outrageous or even out of line, but because she was overspending and debting to get them met, she had become addictive in her spending patterns. She blanked out on the outcomes of her spending until her credit card bills arrived. Month after month, the days preceding her bill due dates had become a nightmare for her. She couldn't sleep, she had chronic indigestion, she chewed her nails to the quick, and she couldn't focus on her work. She was edgy and angry with her boyfriend, and frequently short with customers in her service-industry job.

Alanna and I discussed her priorities, which were:

1. To be able to pay her bills without stress.

2. To be able to travel to see her boyfriend without debt.

3. To save for a "real" trip overseas, specifically a three-month trip to South America.

4. To have money for clothes and fun.

5. To create a Debt-Repayment Plan that didn't ruin her ability to have a good life.

Alanna thought about several strategies, from living very simply at first to pay off small credit cards, to saving very little and allocating as much as she could to living expenses. She chose to take a middle-of-the-road strategy, downsizing obvious overspending, paying minimums on credit cards, and learning to live with reasonable amounts for her wants and needs.

REVIEWING ALANNA'S SECOND-PASS PLAN

Let's take a look at Alanna's second-pass Debt-Free Spending Plan. Note that since her projected expenses were significantly over her income, she had to make multiple changes. But even with lots of down-sized changes, she was still able to find ways to get her needs met less expensively and keep the important elements of her lifestyle in place.

ALANNA'S EDITED SPENDING PLAN (JULY)

Income

July 4 paycheck	$1,447.32
July 18 paycheck	1,447.32
Health Insurance Reimbursement July 1	349.00
Total	$3,243.64

Necessities

Bills	$1,892.61
Daily Needs	935.00
Total	$2,827.61

Balance

$3,243.64 (income) − 2,827.61 (expenses) = $416.03

Note that Alanna's expenses and bills now balance, offering her some cash to put toward Savings, Fun, and meaningful goals.

Savings, Vacation, and Fun Money	**$416.03**
Retirement	(200.00 pretax)
Health Savings Account	(200.00 pretax)
Fun Money	100.00
Healthy Reserve	66.03
Short-Term Savings	80.00
Travel Fund	50.00
Car Repairs	70.00
New Wardrobe Account	25.00
Three Months in South America	25.00
Total	416.03

Though the amounts of money in each account seemed small to Alanna, after only six months she had funded her first wardrobe shopping trip and within one year she had creatively funded her South America trip.

Monthly Plan Detail

Bills	Due	Amount	Former Amount
Rent	1st	572.50	down from 1,145.00
Renter's Insurance	8th	cancelled	down from 45.00
Health Insurance	27th	325.00	
Car Payment	1st	294.00	
Cell Phone	21st	88.00	
Car Insurance	20th	91.00	down from 119.22
Gym	5th	57.00	down from 145.00
Cable	3rd	cancelled	down from 117.55
Visa	20th	254.00 min	
MasterCard	5th	108.11 min	
Kohl's	17th	54.00 min	
JCrew	12th	paid off	down from 49.00
Victoria's Secret	7th	paid off	down from 88.00
Nordstrom	25th	49.00 min	
Total		1,892.61	

Note that Alanna has called her service providers to change her due dates so they work for her Spending Plan. She'll pay most of her bills with the second paycheck in the month.

Daily Needs	Amount	Former Amount
Food (Groceries)	300.00	
Fuel	225.00	
Parking/Tolls/Public Transit	10.00	
Medical Co-Pays	30.00	
Drug Store	35.00	
Beauty/Personal Care	55.00	
Clothing	60.00	down from 100.00
Dry Cleaning	40.00	down from 100.00
Household	30.00	down from 50.00
Postage	10.00	
Haircut	35.00 (save $70 every 2 months)	down from 225.00
Entertainment	20.00	
Plane Flights	0.00	down from 450.00

Dining	50.00	down from 450.00
Massage Therapy	35.00	down from 250.00
Nail Salon	did her own	down from 200.00
Total	935.00	

REVIEWING ALANNA'S EDITED PLAN

The first thing we need to note in Alanna's Spending Plan is how much changed. For those of us who need to downsize significantly, we may find this downsizing daunting at first. But remember that we're going to go to whatever lengths we need to in order to live debt-free. By reviewing the simple changes Alanna made, we can see that the changes really are doable, and that by rethinking our approach, we can keep many of the spending items that are important to us. We just need to think a bit more creatively.

The biggest change Alanna made in her amounts for Bills was to get a roommate for her two-bedroom, utilities-paid, rent-controlled apartment. Though she admitted she would rather live alone, she realized she needed to choose between selling her car (which was not critical, since she walks to work and lives in a city with public transit) and getting a roommate. She chose to keep the freedom of her car and share her living space until she was more solvent and could afford the rent on her own again. (As it turned out, a friend from college was in need of an affordable apartment, and their roommate situation worked quite well.)

Since Alanna kept her car, she also needed to add a Car Repairs Savings account and set aside a monthly allotment to put into that account. Car repairs are one of the easiest ways for debtors to run up credit lines, in that we never plan for them. So Alanna agreed to create and fund this account at the rate of $70 a month.

She then downsized several bills. In addition to paying less rent, she canceled her renter's insurance, canceled the cable in favor of the public library's DVD collection, and joined a gym for $57 a month that offered yoga, canceling her $145 yoga studio membership. She also got a better rate on her car insurance, saving a few dollars. Those changes saved her more than $800. But since she was so far over her income, these changes were not enough.

Alanna had just put $3,000 in the bank—a gift from her parents to help her with her debt—and would have, she admitted, spent it all on clothes and dining if she had not just begun her Spending Plan. She agreed to pay off two small credit card bills with the money—$525 to JCrew and $713 to Victoria's Secret—and she split the remaining $1,762 between her Short-Term Savings account and her Healthy Reserve. She then had two fewer bills—which made her feel terrific—and some cash stashed for unexpected needs. We also note that she was saving some pretax dollars for Retirement and Health Savings, so she wrote that into her Spending Plan to acknowledge the accomplishment of saving.

But the real changes—the changes that would save her from debting—came in reworking her Daily Needs amounts. Alanna's trouble areas were overspending on clothes, dining, travel, and luxuries like expensive massages, haircuts, and nail appointments. She didn't see how she could get any of these needs and wants met if she lived within her means. After a little ingenuity, though, she was able to cover all of them.

First, she went to a massage school once a month that charged $35 a visit with no tipping. She found a reasonable hairdresser who worked out of her home and got a haircut every two months for $70, including tip. She agreed to do her own nails for a short time, until she paid off another small department-store card, but could use any "leftover" cash from her Spending Plan for an affordable nail salon. She allotted $60 a month for clothes and agreed to go shopping once a month with the cash, staying out of expensive clothing stores.

Since Alanna also had created a wardrobe fund and had Fun Money of $100 a month, she could use any of that money for clothes as well. After six months she was able to go outlet shopping with her wardrobe fund, which satisfied her taste for higher-end buying. She found a hip, second-hand clothing store and went in regularly with $20 to blow from her clothing or Fun Money allotment, shopping just for fun. She downsized dry cleaning by doing her laundry rather than sending it out, and she bought household items at a cheaper store.

The biggest change she made was the hardest one: She had to tell her out-of-town boyfriend that she couldn't pay for plane tickets three or four times a month. In fact, she couldn't afford the tickets at all, unless she sold her car. Most of her dining money was also spent on these weekends, running up her credit cards to "fairly" split the cost with him for expensive dinners out. Since he had a high-paying job, she had been embarrassed to tell him that she made significantly less and couldn't afford their weekend lifestyle. The couple had never talked about money, and her boyfriend had believed that she could afford what she was offering.

The upshot was that Alanna's honesty brought the couple closer. Her boyfriend made the effort to visit her for the next year, which was a significant shift in their dynamic, since Alanna had been making all of the travel efforts, and the couple regularly discussed what she could afford to contribute toward their entertainment when he visited. They both got along so much better that within a year they moved in together, creating a clear Debt-Free Spending Plan that covered moving expenses, transition expenses, and their now-settled-in daily-life expenses. Because they were able to have a frank and honest conversation about how to live within their means, the course of their relationship changed, and they were able to take an important step in their commitment.

Lastly, after just one year, by using her Short-Term Savings and her travel account, Alanna was able to fund a plane ticket to Chile, where she joined a volunteer house-building project. The program paid for all of her housing and food for three weeks while the group traveled the coast, repairing and building homes for poorer families. Alanna said that the experience "changed her forever," and helped her respect and value her money, her work, and her life.

REVIEWING ALANNA'S BILL-PAYING PLAN

Since Alanna gets paid every two weeks, she also needs a Bill-Paying Plan so she knows which bills to pay with each check. While this might seem like a tedious extra step, it's an imperative one for those of us who blank out on how to distribute our cash *as it comes in*. The few finance books I researched that did offer monthly money worksheets stopped short of this step. Since we debtors tune out on our money, we need a road map showing not only what we have and what we can spend but *when* we can spend it.

Remember that if you get paid on July 4, then your Daily Needs spending for the month of July is not going to start until that date, unless you're ahead of the paycheck game—and most of us debtors are not. So, you make a Bill-Paying Plan that tells you when to pay your Bills, when you can use your Daily Needs cash, and when you can fund your Savings accounts.

Note that we always try to fund all of our Daily Needs in our first paycheck if we can. Why do we need to do that? As discussed in Chapter 3, we want to be able to put all of our Daily Needs amounts into our Magic Little Notebook at the first of the month, if we can. It gives us a good feeling to know that our needs are allotted for and taken care of. And it's a bit less math. So, in Alanna's case, she changed some of her due dates so that she could pay the majority of her Bills with her second paycheck of the month, and fund her Daily Needs with her first one.

What we're creating here is a road map for spending that's clear as a bell. That means we'll know exactly the next move we're making financially, even if it's just when to pay which bill.

ALANNA'S BILL-PAYING PLAN

July 1 Health Insurance Reimbursement	+349.00
July 4 Paycheck	+1,447.32
Total	+1,796.32

July 4 Pays For:	Due Date	$1,796.32
Daily Needs		935.00
Rent	1st	572.50
Gym	5th	57.00
MasterCard	5th	108.11 min
Total		1,672.61
		123.71 rolls over to next check

Note that the extra $123.71 stays in Alanna's account to add to her next check for bill paying—it's not for spending. Her spending comes only from her allotted Daily Needs amounts. We don't randomly spend what's in our accounts without referencing our Spending Plan.

Rollover from last check		+123.71
July 18 Paycheck		+1,447.32
Total		+1,571.03

July 18 Pays for:	Due Date	+1,571.03
Savings, Vacation, Fun	18th	416.03
Health Insurance	27th	325.00
Car Payment	1st	294.00 (pay at end of month for the 1st)
Cell Phone	21st	88.00
Car Insurance	20th	91.00
Visa	20th	254.00 min
Kohl's	17th	54.00 min
Nordstrom	25th	49.00 min
Total		1,571.03

In Alanna's Bill-Paying Plan, we note that since she is not ahead of the bill-paying game, she will pay her rent a couple of days late, on the fourth. Since her paycheck is automatically deposited, she can reasonably drop her rent check in the landlord's box the night of the 3rd. She's not going to play roulette with her checking account—if she's a couple of days late on the rent until she catches up, so be it. Her Kohl's bill also might be a day late. But we don't worry about that. We just get as close as possible and do the best we can. Alanna's Bill-Paying Plan tells her when to start using the Daily Needs totals in her Magic Little Notebook, and when to pay each bill so she doesn't get confused.

Note that if our money is really close to the bone, then we need a Bill-Paying Plan to help us allocate our money. The easiest thing to do when we're starting out is to get so enthusiastic about paying our bills on time that we pay them too soon and screw up our living-expense money. So map out your Bill-Paying Plan and live by it. It will help you know which money moves to make next—even when you're busy—and that will help you to relax.

Pete's Debt-Free Spending Plan

Following is Pete's first-pass attempt at a Debt-Free Spending Plan, with notes and comments to help explain the details. Note that though Pete is making a very healthy salary, he's still spending over his income by more than $1,900 each month. Given that he has two college-bound children and no savings, and a depreciated investment in his home, his accrued monthly debt is seriously detrimental to his and his family's future. In addition, Pete and his wife divorced, in part, over money and spending issues.

PETE'S FIRST-PASS SPENDING PLAN (JULY)

Income

July 4 paycheck	$5,442.00
July 24 paycheck	5,442.00
Sales Bonus	(ranges $500–1,000 typically)
Total	$10,884.00

Necessities

Bills	$9,209.78
Daily Needs	3,575.00
Total	12,784.78

Balance

$10,884.00 (income) − 12,784.78 (expenses) = $−1,900.78

Note that Pete is $1,900.78 over his income each month in this Spending Plan. Though he brings home more than $10,000 a month, his overages have been accruing on credit cards, accounting for his $80,000+ debt.

Savings, Vacation, and Fun Money	+0.00
Fun Money	0.00
Healthy Reserve	0.00
Short-Term Savings	0.00
College Fund for kids	0.00
Wedding Fund for daughter	0.00
New Car Savings Account	0.00
Vacation Account	0.00
Total	0.00

Since Pete is negative in his monthly spending, he can't fund any of the priority areas he identified as savings needs.

Monthly Plan Detail

Bills	Due	Amount
Mortgage	3rd	3,974.00
Homeowner's Insurance	17th	267.00
PG&E Utilities	20th	230.00
Water & Garbage	25th	52.00
Kids' School Tuition	4th	1,257.00
Health Insurance	7th	825.00
Car Payment	5th	594.00
Cell Phone	15th	99.00
Car Insurance	10th	101.34 auto deduct
Gym	1st	175.00
Netflix	1st	44.00
Cable	3rd	123.44
Visa	10th	328.00 min
MasterCard	20th	250.00 min
Credit line	4th	659.00 min
Gap	10th	34.00 min
Banana Republic	15th	29.00 min

Sears	25th	47.00 min
Best Buy	23rd	121.00 min
Total		9,209.78

Daily Needs	**Amount**
Food (Groceries)	450.00
Fuel	325.00
Parking/Tolls/Public Transit	40.00
Medical Co-Pays	30.00
Drug Store	45.00
Beauty/Personal Care	55.00
Clothing	150.00
Dry Cleaning	80.00
Household	50.00
Postage	10.00
Haircut	170.00
Entertainment	20.00
Golf	525.00
Dining	925.00
Cash Contributions	700.00
Total	3,575.00

REVIEWING PETE'S FIRST-PASS PLAN

Note that in Pete's ballparked Spending Plan, he's over his income by $1,900.78. Though he takes home over $10,000 a month, he's still been able to rack up more than $80,000 in debt by living beyond his means. In this first-pass Spending Plan, he's also not accounting for upcoming spending items, like trips, summer camps for his kids, athletic gear, and toys (including a new big-screen TV)—all recently paid for with credit cards and all adding to his balances.

Pete is "successful" by all counts—he has a big, expensive house; he sends his two sons to a private school; he takes his family out to dinner; and he picks up the tab for his friends. He golfs regularly, contributes to his church, and owns a brand-new car. The problem is that Pete is always stressed; he's been having trouble sleeping, and that has contributed to a serious spike in his blood pressure this year.

His house isn't worth what he paid for it, his kids will be nearing college in a few short years and he has no savings for their schooling, and his debts are mounting. Worse yet, his sales have been slipping at work, and he's constantly worried. Pete and his wife split up two years earlier, brought about in part by their arguing over mounting debt and money issues.

Pete and I discussed his priorities, which were:

1. His health.

2. Learning to pay for things in cash, including vacations.

3. His kids' college education.

4. Saving for his oldest daughter's wedding in two years.

Pete weighed several options. He could keep his Bills at status quo and downsize his Daily Needs enough to live debt-free, but that would leave little for savings. Or, he could make some significant changes to his lifestyle to cut his Bills, and start stashing some cash in special Savings accounts.

Although Pete also sometimes earns up to $1,000 more than his base salary each month, that amount is not guaranteed and has dropped as low as $300 recently. So, Pete agreed that he needed a separate strategy to deal with his bonus money.

REVIEWING PETE'S SECOND-PASS PLAN

On Pete's second pass through his Debt-Free Spending Plan, he was able to change his spending to bring it into line with both his priorities and his income. His edited Spending Plan looks like this:

PETE'S EDITED SPENDING PLAN (JULY)

Income

July 4 paycheck	$5,442.00
July 24 paycheck	5,442.00
Sales Bonus	(ranges $500–$1,000 typically)
Total	$10,884.00

Note that we're not including Pete's bonus money in his Spending Plan because it's not a regular amount of money that can be relied upon. Instead, we developed a separate Spending Plan for his bonus money, listed below.

Necessities

Bills	$6,701.15
Daily Needs	1,940.00
Total	$8,641.15

Balance

$10,884.00 (income) − 8,641.15 (expenses) = $ 2,242.85

Note that Pete now has $2,242.85 left over after his funding his expenses to put toward his Savings and Fun Money.

Savings, Vacation, and Fun	$2,242.85
Fun Money	250.00
Healthy Reserve	275.00
Short-Term Savings	225.00
College Fund for kids	1,000.00
Wedding Fund for daughter	200.00
New Car Savings Account	50.00
Vacation Account	242.85
Total	2,242.85

By downsizing and making some clear money decisions, Pete is now in the black, funding some things in cash that are meaningful to him.

Monthly Plan Detail

Bills	Due	Amount	Former Amount
Mortgage	3rd	3,974.00	
Homeowner's insurance	17th	233.00	down from 267.00
PG&E Utilities	20th	230.00	
Water & Garbage	25th	52.00	
Kids' School Tuition	4th	0.00	down from 1,257.00
Health Insurance	7th	613.00	down from 825.00

Car Payment	5th	0.00	down from 594.00
Cell Phone	15th	99.00	
Car Insurance	10th	65.15	down from 101.34
Gym	1st	44.00	down from 175.00
Netflix	1st	44.00	
Cable	3rd	0.00	down from 123.44
Visa	10th	328.00 min	
MasterCard	20th	250.00 min	
Credit line	4th	659.00 min	
Gap	10th	34.00 min	
Banana Republic	15th	29.00 min	
Sears	25th	47.00 min	
Best Buy	23rd	0.00	down from 121.00 min
Total		6,701.15	down from 9,209.78

Note that by making some simple changes in his Bills, Pete was able to redirect more than $2,000 in living-expense cash.

Daily Needs	Amount	Former Amount
Food (Groceries)	650.00	up from 450.00
Fuel	325.00	
Parking/Tolls/ Public Transit	40.00	
Medical Co-Pays	30.00	
Drug Store	45.00	
Beauty/ Personal Care	55.00	
Clothing	195.00	up from 150.00
Dry Cleaning	80.00	
Household	50.00	
Postage	10.00	
Haircut	20.00	down from 170.00
Entertainment	240.00	up from 20.00
Golf	0.00	down from 525.00
Dining	100.00	down from 925.00
Cash Contributions	100.00	down from 700.00
Total	1,940.00	down from 3,575.00

Note that not all of Pete's categories had to be adjusted down. Food and entertainment were increased, while out-of-proportion expenses were decreased to free up more cash.

REVIEWING PETE'S EDITED PLAN

Let's review the changes that Pete made to have his Spending Plan work for him. After making three or four passes, Pete realized that if he was to make any significant cash contribution to his twin sons' college education, he would have to make some significant cuts. That meant either selling his house and buying something less expensive or sending his kids to a public school.

Since the value of his home had recently dropped, selling wasn't a great short-term choice. He sat his sons down and talked to them about the decision. His sons had friends in the neighborhood entering the public high school the next year, and as it turned out, they were not bothered significantly by the decision to change to a public school. He told his sons that he was making every effort to live debt-free and wanted them to have the benefit of some cash to attend college when the time came.

That decision saved Pete $1,257 a month. With that adjustment and a few small changes, he could have made up his deficit, but his goal was to free up even more cash. He had several savings needs that were more important to him than having more monthly spending cash. First, he got a better rate on his homeowners insurance, changed to an HMO instead of a PPO for his family's health care, and since his sons were big movie fans, kept the bigger Netflix plan and canceled the cable. His kids also taught him how to stream movies and sports programs online, which made letting go of cable even easier.

His cell phone plan was reasonable, so he kept it, but his gym was obviously overpriced, so he switched to a much cheaper neighborhood gym. Though he had recently bought a new car, he had two paid-for vehicles in the driveway—an older BMW and a truck. He sold the new car, got a low insurance rate on his older ones, and opened a Savings account for a new car, agreeing to wait until his Spending Plan was under control before he bought again. Since he agreed to put a significant amount into his Short-Term Savings account each month, Pete decided to use that account for car repairs, as well as other unexpected items, and a short while later he added another Savings account specifically for his cars.

Pete's monthly credit card payments were very high when he began his Spending Plan—more than $1,400 a month. When Pete saw on paper what he was actually paying in debt repayment, he decided to take the month-old big-screen TV back to Best Buy and cancel the debt he had incurred. (The family already had three large TVs in the house before the new purchase.) By making these changes, Pete was able to save $2,083.63 on his Bills.

Next, he tackled his Daily Needs. At first glance, he knew that spending more than $900 a month on dining out when he was in serious debt trouble was like adding gasoline to a raging fire. He decided to create a special category for dining out, allotting $100 to take his sons out for dinner once a month, and funded a general entertainment category at $240 a month. He increased his grocery amounts to cover more meals at home, then allotted a generous amount to his Fun Money category—$250—money he could use for anything he chose, including dining out.

Since most often Pete's entertainment choice was to go to a movie and dinner with his sons, he then had three pools of money to draw from. He stopped going out to group dinners with friends, preferring instead to host barbeques in his backyard, covered by his grocery or Fun Money.

After the first month of trying to live with his Spending Plan, Pete noticed an amazing thing. His boys got into the spirit of the family's living within their means, and they started planning events based on what Pete had to spend each month. It became a project for his sons to figure out how many entertainment outings they could fund, and it took the pressure off of Pete. Instead of feeling as if he were taking something away from his kids, he ended up feeling that he was sharing a valuable lesson—something he never learned from his own parents.

Note that though Pete's Savings categories are not huge, they are significant in relation to his past debting and lack of savings. Over time, Pete started saving significant amounts more as he lived within his means, and that gave him immense pride and a greater willingness to live within his Spending Plan. And since he was not debting and adding to his credit card balances, he was able to see real progress in his debt reduction. Though we're not going to review it here, Pete also created a Bill-Paying Plan based on his twice-monthly paychecks. (Please see the Alanna example earlier in the chapter for details on how to create one.)

THE ONE-THIRD RULE FOR WINDFALL MONEY

So what did we do with Pete's bonus money? Pete had been averaging $500 to $1,000 per month in bonus money, but recently that amount had dropped as low as $300. We decided to treat it as "windfall money," and apply the One-Third Rule. That is, with any money that comes in over and above our regular, stable income, one-third goes to debt repayment, one-third goes to savings, and one-third is extra spending cash. Cash gifts, money gifts from parents, bonuses, tax refunds, et cetera can all be considered windfall money.

In Pete's case, his bonus amounts are not folded into his regular Spending Plan, but they augment them. The One-Third Rule allowed Pete to pay off several of his smaller department-store accounts within three or four months, freeing up more cash for his monthly Spending Plan. He applied one-third to his debt (paying off smaller cards first), one-third to his chosen Savings accounts, and one-third for cash spending. This allowed a little extra cash to fund gifts or special things for his kids—extras like summer camps, sporting team costs, or a few rounds of golf. After six months, Pete had paid off all of his smaller cards and had reduced one larger credit card balance by about 25 percent.

Michaela's Debt-Free Spending Plan

Michaela had an administrative assistant job for a human services agency when we first met, and she was making $49,000 a year. She had more than $14,000 in debt from overspending—not a lot by debtor standards, but significant in relation to her income. She was also in danger of losing her job owing to downsizing. Most of her debt overages came from paying for expensive therapy and buying things for her needy, unemployed mother. Michaela had recently separated from her live-in fiancée, in part because they argued about money. Let's take a look at her first-pass Spending Plan.

MICHAELA'S FIRST-PASS SPENDING PLAN (JULY)

Income	
July 1	$2,832.00
Necessities	
Bills	$1,833.55
Daily Needs	918.00
Total	$2,751.55
Balance	
$ 2,832.00 (income) − 2,751.55 (expenses) = $80.45	

Note that, though Michaela's Spending Plan balances, it does not include the expenses she covers for her mother on credit cards, which average $400 to $600 a month.

Savings, Vacation, and Fun	**$80.45**
Fun & Entertainment Money	25.00
Healthy Reserve	10.00
Short-Term Savings Account	20.00
Photography Classes	15.00
Travel Account	10.45
Total	80.45

Even though her income is not large, she is still able to allocate small amounts to all of her savings accounts.

Monthly Plan Detail

Bills	Due	Amount
Rent	4th	1,100.75
Health Insurance	n/a	covered by company
Car Payment	12th	247.00
Car Insurance	3rd	139.00
Cell Phone	16th	99.00
Electric	17th	35.00 (pay $70.00 every other month)
Gas, Utilities	15th	22.00
Gym	1st	27.00
Movie Subscription	3rd	8.39
Savings	1st	25.00
Student Loan	1st	50.41
Citicard	17th	80.00 minimum
Total		1,833.55

None of Michaela's Bills are overly large, and the amounts are in relative proportion to her cash income—which means that her debting comes from overspending on Daily Needs, impulse debting, and expenses outside her Spending Plan.

Daily Needs	Amount
Food	250.00
Coffee	25.00
Lunches	50.00
Fuel/Parking	200.00
Doctor Visits	covered
Drug Store	30.00
Beauty/Personal	20.00
Dry Cleaners	25.00
Laundry Home (coin ops)	30.00
Household	20.00
Postage	8.00

Haircut	20.00
Dining out	100.00
Therapy	120.00
Clothing	20.00
Total	918.00

Since one of Michaela's debting downfalls is dining out on credit, she agreed to allocate $100 to dining so she wouldn't feel compelled to debt. All of her other expenses are in proportion to her income.

REVIEWING MICHAELA'S FIRST-PASS PLAN

Before we met to work on her Debt-Free Spending Plan, Michaela had already done a lot of the legwork, downsizing her monthly spending. For her Bills, she got rid of her home phone and her home Internet (since she didn't really use her computer at home) in favor of a smartphone with net access. Then she downsized her movie subscription.

Since none of her other Bills were exceptionally high, she moved on to her Daily Needs. She found a more affordable hair stylist, and cut spending on postage, dry cleaning, and clothing (not a priority for her). She had been spending up to $500 a month on therapy—an expense not in alignment with her income. She was able to find a neighborhood women's clinic that offered therapy for $30 a visit, and limited herself to four visits per month for a total of $120 per month. Though she felt attached to her previous therapist, she was able to choose a new one at the women's clinic that she ended up loving.

Given that she also had a tendency to debt when she went to restaurants, and also for coffees and lunches, she agreed to allot reasonable amounts to each of these areas—amounts that would make her feel like she was not depriving herself. She decided to put small amounts into her Savings, at least until she got the hang of living debt-free.

Though her first-pass attempt balanced debt-free, Michaela's biggest challenge was not represented in her Spending Plan. She was most compromised financially by trying to fund her unemployed mother's needs—expenses that Michaela was trying to provide for on her small salary. These costs often went on her credit cards, amounting to between $400 and $600 a month. We had an honest conversation in which we discussed how she was sacrificing her financial stability for her mother, and how that compromised her future, as well as her ability to focus on finding work she loved or could live with.

Given her mother's dependency on her, it was not easy for Michaela to tell her mother that she wouldn't be supporting her anymore, and wouldn't be paying for groceries, bills, and so on. Her mother was not pleased, and she attempted to guilt Michaela into continuing to give her money. But Michaela held her ground, told her mother that she had been debting to cover expenses, and could no longer help her. After just a month, she felt a huge weight lifted off of her shoulders, and was able to focus on her job search. Though her mother continued to call her up with money "emergencies" and desperate requests, Michaela held firm, saying simply each time, "I'm sorry, but I can't give you money or pay for things for you anymore." If she chose to give her mom a gift, she agreed she would cut out her coffee or downsize her dining-out money, but she no longer was the go-to girl for her mom's inability to fund her own life.

Six months later, Michaela had taken the professional photography course she had her eye on, and she began shooting portraits and events on weekends, earning $500 for each shoot. She didn't lose her job, but a year later, she was able to move to a part-time job in a photography gallery, funding the rest of her needs with her growing photography business. Her life took both a financial and an emotional upturn, and in three years, even with a modest income, Michaela had paid off all of her debts—a feat she'd never been able to accomplish in her adult life.

Jake and Anna's Debt-Free Spending Plan

Now, let's take a look at a couple's Debt-Free Spending Plan. Jake and Anna had been putting their cash into two separate accounts, and then Jake would (often belatedly) pay the Bills, and ask Anna for a check for half of them. Then they each spent randomly for themselves and the family, using their credit cards liberally for anything they couldn't fund with cash. This strategy had left them more than $50,000 in debt, with no assets or savings.

Since their two children were in third and fifth grade, respectively, and both were very bright, they knew that they should be funding a College account, but hadn't begun to because of their debt. They also both longed to buy a house for their family, but had no idea how to fund a down payment.

Let's take a look at Jake and Anna's first-pass Spending Plan. Note that their Couple's Spending Plan lists their needs jointly, the way they've been managing them, and their revised Spending Plan is split into two to help them share the responsibility of their finances.

JAKE AND ANNA'S FIRST-PASS SPENDING PLAN (JULY)

Income

Jake	$2,815.00
Anna, July 1	1,633.21
Anna, July 15	1,633.21
Total	$6,081.42

Necessities

Bills	$4,955.00
Daily Needs	2,400.00
Total	$7,355.00

Balance

$6,081.42 (income) − 7,355.00 (expenses) = $−1,273.58

Note that the couple is spending $1,273.58 more than their cash income each month. They also add to their debt totals for things like sports equipment, toys, vacations, clothes, and general household expenses.

Savings, Vacation, and Fun	0.00
Fun & Entertainment Money	0.00
Healthy Reserve	0.00
Short-Term Savings Account	0.00
Car Repairs	0.00
Kids' College Account	0.00
Kids' Sports & Music Account	0.00
Vacation Account	0.00
Total	0.00

Note that since Jake and Anna are overspending and debting, they have no cash to fund their wants and priority savings needs.

Monthly Plan Detail

Bills	Due	Amount
Rent	1st	2,288.00
Utilities	15th	72.00 (gas, electric)
Water & garbage	3rd	54.00
Health Insurance	1st	477.00
After-school care	1st	650.00
Rx (monthly)	1st	45.00
Car 1	7th	224.00
Car 2	12th	378.00
Car insurance	10th	107.00
Cable	14th	129.00
Gym	10th	99.00
Newspaper 1	1st	45.00
Newspaper 2	1st	55.00
Frye's	7th	31.00
Visa	3rd	189.00
MNBA	18th	112.00
Parents' loan	1st	not paying yet
Total		4,955.00

Daily Needs	Amount
Food	550.00
Coffee	100.00
Lunches, Anna & David	150.00

School Lunches, kids	175.00
Fuel/Parking	425.00
Doctor Visits	60.00
Drug Store	30.00
Dry Cleaners	100.00
Postage	35.00
Dining out	100.00
Clothing, Family	400.00
Clothing, Anna	200.00
Dog Food	75.00
Total	2,400.00

Though many of their needs are not out of proportion for a family of four, there are specific areas that can be downsized to free up cash to help them to live debt-free.

REVIEWING JAKE AND ANNA'S FIRST-PASS PLAN

Since Jake works for the Parks and Recreation Department and gets paid once a month, it's very clear what he has to contribute to the family's living expenses each month. Anna has a 30-hour-a-week job as a bank teller, and gets paid twice a month, though she often gets income from working extra weekend hours. Anna hands over her check to Jake, claiming she's "no good with math or money." Jake, though, often "forgets" when their bills are due and has run up a bunch of late fees for the couple over the past two years. Both use credit cards liberally for whatever they feel they "need."

Though their rent is not way out of line for a small suburban house in a metropolitan area, and neither are most of their Bills and Daily Needs, they still have to find ways to downsize in order to live free from debt. Their first-pass Spending Plan did not address several areas of need that the couple had: kids' soccer costs, music lessons for their daughter, summer camps, and other child-related expenses they had been putting on credit cards. It also did not cover vacations, car repairs, Short-Term Savings, or a Healthy Reserve.

Since their money was tight, Anna and Jake decided to postpone saving for a house until they paid down some of their debts.

In addition, they were regularly spending an average of $250 a month on veterinarian bills for both of their pets. Since one animal had kidney disease and another had diabetes—and they had never planned for vet expenses, always treating them as if they were unexpected—all of their vet bills had ended up going on credit cards.

When I suggested that they put $250 a month aside for their pets, they were slightly horrified. "How can we do that? We just can't afford it!" they said. When I noted that they were spending that money already, and that it was fine to make their animals a priority in their lives, they still had a hard time accepting the amount they needed to fund their pets. But since they both knew they needed to learn to live debt-free, they agreed to add some cash to a Pet Savings account in their revised Spending Plan.

Lastly, Jake had borrowed $20,000 from his parents to pay off his credit card debt eight years earlier and had not been paying it back. The couple agreed to start adding a payback amount to their Bills each month.

REVIEWING JAKE AND ANNA'S EDITED PLAN

Note that in Jake and Anna's second pass, they divided up their family's Bills and Daily Needs spending between the two of them, constructing a separate Debt-Free Spending Plan for each of them. This immediately took the pressure off of Jake, who had been resenting his role as the "responsible" bill payer and keep-it-all-together financial partner.

The object of splitting up the Bills and Daily Needs spending was not to make private each spouse's spending; they still met each month and went over their total amounts as a couple. What it was designed to do was to more equally distribute the responsibility for the couple's finances, which only helped them both gain ownership of their joint spending and bill paying.

Since Jake got paid once a month, he decided to call all of his providers and get his bill due-dates changed to the fifth or the sixth of the month. That way he could sit down at the first of the month, pay all his Bills, and not have to think about them again for thirty days. These two changes—sharing the bill paying and changing his due dates—gave him immediate relief. Next, the couple agreed that Anna needed to be responsible for some of the family's Daily Needs, as well as some Bills, to be a fully participating partner in their joint finances.

Let's take a look at the changes they made. First, we review Jake's Spending Plan, and then we review Anna's. Note that the couple made decisions together about how to divide up the duties and the cash they had, and then gave each other the autonomy to manage his or her part.

JAKE'S EDITED SPENDING PLAN (JULY)

Income	
Jake	$2,815.00
Necessities	
Bills	$1,219.00
Daily Needs	1,200.00
Total	$2,419.00
Balance	

$2,815.00 (income) − 2,419.00 (expenses) = $396.00

Savings, Vacation, and Fun	**$396.00**
Fun & Entertainment Money	200.00
Healthy Reserve (joint)	40.00
Short-Term Savings Account (joint)	55.00
Car Repairs	81.00
Sport Bike	20.00
Total	396.00

Note that since Jake is now in the black, he can put cash aside for the things that are meaningful to the couple and to himself—including cash to fund a secret desire to own a sport bike.

Monthly Plan Detail

Bills	Due	Amount	Former Amount
Utilities	5th	72.00	
Water & Garbage	3rd	54.00	
Health Insurance	6th	477.00	
After-school Care	5th	n/a	down from 650.00
Car 2	12th	378.00	
Car Insurance	10th	107.00	
Pet Insurance	6th	50.00	
Cable	n/a	cancelled	down from 129.00
Gym	n/a	cancelled	down from 99.00
Newspaper 1	n/a	cancelled	down from 45.00
Newspaper 2	n/a	cancelled	down from 55.00
Frye's	7th	31.00	
Parents' Loan	1st	50.00	
Total		1,219.00	

Jake's Spending Plan significantly simplified his bill paying, which meant he no longer resented having to pay them.

Daily Needs	Amount	Former Amount
Food	600.00	up from 550.00
Coffee	n/a	down from 100.00 for two
Lunches	25.00	down from 150.00 for two
School Lunches, kids	50.00	down from 175.00
Fuel/Parking	225.00	split from 425.00
Doctor Visits	30.00	down from 60.00 for two
Drug Store	30.00	
Dry Cleaners	25.00	down from 100.00
Postage	10.00	down from 35.00
Dining out	100.00	
Clothing, Family	to Anna	down from 400.00
Clothing, Jake	60.00	
Dog Food	45.00	down from 75.00
Total	1,200.00	

REVIEWING JAKE'S EDITED PLAN

First, Anna and Jake needed to do some juggling to figure out which partner paid for which Bills. They divided up the Bills based on how much money each of them was bringing in monthly or bi-monthly, and then divided up Daily Needs expenses for the family. They made sure that each of them could put money aside for Fun and for Savings after paying Bills and Daily Needs. That meant they had to make some cuts.

At first glance, Jake and Anna thought that they should be able to keep many of the things that they ended up cutting—things like their cable service. But when they honestly looked at their numbers, they knew something had to give. Once they admitted that they couldn't keep everything they wanted, they canceled both newspapers, canceled the gym in favor of walking together, and canceled the cable. Since Jake was a huge sports fan, the couple agreed to set aside enough Fun Money so that Jake could meet up with friends at a pub to watch big games.

Jake works in a casual environment that doesn't require wearing a suit, so he agreed to downsize his $100 for dry cleaning (it was all his expense) to $25 a month. The couple was also spending $425 a month on coffee, lunches out, and kids' school lunches—expenses they agreed they really could not afford—so they decided to cut those dramatically.

They bought a coffee maker and made coffee at home; they made lunches for work and the kids' lunches. Surprising to both of them, lunch making became a fun after-dinner time for their family. After they finished dinner, they turned up the music, cleaned the kitchen, and made lunches together, laughing and goofing off. Each family member made his or her own lunch, but they did it all together. This took the pressure off of Anna, and she began to feel better about her responsibilities to the family's Spending Plan. Note that their grocery money went up from $500 to $600—a reasonable increase to cover the added food for lunches. They allotted $50 a month for their kids to have lunch at school on Friday "hot dog days," which the kids loved.

Their hardest decision was how to deal with their pets' veterinary bills. Since they really did not have an extra $250 in their plan each month to cover high vet bills, they agreed to fund pet health insurance at $50 a month. They also agreed that they could use their co-pays categories to fund the vet co-pays, as well as family medical co-pays. Finally, they agreed that they would fund whatever was covered by their veterinary policy, and nothing more, and would not go into debt for high-cost surgeries or therapies for their animals.

REVIEWING ANNA'S SECOND-PASS PLAN

One of Anna and Jake's biggest expenses was after-school child care, which felt like a major necessity to them both. With a little bit of discussion, they agreed that Jake could shift his work hours to 7:00 a.m. to 3:00 p.m., and pick up the kids after school, which would allow them to save $650 a month on after-school care. Anna would be responsible for getting the kids to school in the mornings, and Jake, who did most of the cooking, could have afternoons to be with the kids and get dinner ready.

To make this change stick, they agreed that Anna would get up at 6:00 a.m. with Jake, and would not stay up later than he did in the evenings. In other words, they made a family choice that supported their financial choice. This relieved the family of a major expense that helped them to live debt-free, and it was critical in making both of their Spending Plans balance.

Let's look at how that change affected Anna's Spending Plan.

ANNA'S EDITED SPENDING PLAN (JULY)

Income

Anna, July 1	$1,633.21
Anna, July 15	1,633.21
Anna, Overtime	(see below)
Total	$3,266.42

Necessities

Bills	$2,823.00
Daily Needs	400.00
Total	$3,223.00

Balance

$3,266.42 (income) − 3,223.00 (expenses) = $43.42

Note that Anna is funding her savings accounts from her overtime money, which varies. She manages this by transferring any cash over her base pay ($1,633.21) into her respective savings accounts.

Savings, Vacation, and Fun	**+43.42**
Fun & Entertainment Money	43.42 from balance above

Extra Income

Weekend Overtime (ranges $175–$200 each paycheck)

Each time Anna gets paid, she'll divide her overtime money into the following accounts. She set up several Savings accounts, attached them to her checking account, and can easily transfer amounts to savings online.

July 1 paycheck, Overtime Money	**$179.15**
Healthy Reserve (joint)	30.00
Short-Term Savings Account (joint)	49.15
Kids' College Account	40.00
Kids' Sports & Music Account	25.00
Vacation Account	35.00
Total	179.15

July 15 paycheck, Overtime Money	**$158.13**
Healthy Reserve (joint)	20.00
Short-Term Savings Account (joint)	20.00
Kids' College Account	40.00
Kids' Sports & Music Account	20.00
Vacation Account	58.13
Total	158.13

Note that Anna can vary the percentage she puts into each account, for simplicity's sake. The point is that she puts anything over her base pay ($1,633.21) into her Savings accounts and divides up the money as she chooses.

Monthly Plan Detail

Bills	Due	Amount	Former Amount
Rent	1st	2,288.00	
Rx (monthly)	1st	10.00	45.00
After-school Care	1st	n/a	down from 650.00
Car 1	7th	224.00	
Visa	3rd	189.00	
MNBA	18th	112.00	
Total		2,823.00	

Daily Needs	Amount	Former Amount
Food	25.00	
Coffee	0.00	down from 100.00
Lunches	25.00	down from 150.00
Fuel/Parking	150.00	
Doctor Visits	40.00	
Drug Store	25.00	
Dry Cleaners	25.00	100.00 for two
Postage	10.00	
Clothing, Kids	50.00	
Clothing, Anna	50.00	down from 200.00
Total	400.00	

REVIEWING ANNA'S EDITED PLAN

The first thing we note about Anna's Spending Plan is that she funds her Savings with her overtime. By building in a structure that covers her expenses with her base pay, Anna can then use her variable overtime to fund her Savings accounts. This system works only because she has *regular* overtime. (If she only got overtime once in a while, then we would treat it like "windfall money"; see Pete's example, above.)

Anna made some simple cuts, like getting a generic version of her medication each month, cutting out the coffee bar, and allotting $25 for eating lunch out each month. Since her co-workers like to socialize and celebrate birthdays together, she used that money for those occasions. She told her co-workers that she could only afford $25 a month for these events—that meant out-the-door, including tip. She first felt embarrassed by having to set that financial boundary, but later two of her co-workers thanked her for helping to cap overpriced lunches that none of them could really afford.

Though the couple had agreed that Jake would do the grocery shopping (since he's the cook), realistically, Anna often ended up picking up little things from the grocery store for him on her way home from work. She put aside $25 to cover those items. In other words, though she was downsizing, she still made her Spending Plan work for her realistic needs.

Since clothing was a big deal for Anna—and a major source of debting—she had a hard time accepting that she wouldn't be able to debt to buy clothes when she saw them. She agreed to shop at inexpensive stores and to not hold on to her clothing money for longer than two months. Since she liked buying clothes, it was important that she buy them—she just needed to live within her allotted $50 a month. After she realized that she would always have $50 *each month* for clothes, and when she realized she would feel no guilt when she bought them, she was able to stick to her Spending Plan. She also could use her Fun Money, any extra birthday money, or any Daily Needs cash she didn't use to fund clothing purchases. After a year she added another Savings account for herself specifically for clothing.

Lastly, since Anna got paid twice a month, she also created a Bill-Paying Plan (see Chapter 3 and the Alanna example, above) so that she was crystal clear when her family bills were due and which check they came out of.

After using their Debt-Free Spending Plans for four months, Anna and Jake noticed some terrific things. First, they felt better about themselves—"like real grownups," Anna said. Second, they had stopped fighting about money. When they had a money decision to discuss and the temperature started to rise, one of them would say, "Let's just look at the numbers."

Since they were fighting less and felt less stressed, their kids sensed the added ease in the house and seemed to be better adjusted. A small behavioral problem their son had earlier had cleared up, and the siblings began getting along better. They weren't overspending on entertainment or events, so they began spending more time outdoors on bikes and hiking together, which all four agreed had changed their family for the better.

David and Ellie's Debt-Free Spending Plan

Let's review a more complicated couple's Spending Plan. David and Ellie had several large challenges in their financial life. First, Ellie works part time as a social worker on a variable shift. Though she loves her work, the pay is not high, barely balancing out their child-care costs. David, by turns, has worked as an entrepreneur and consultant to software start-up companies, which pays erratically. Recently he has also invested with a venture capital group that buys depreciated properties and attempts to repair and flip them. David suffers from a medical condition that has cost the couple up to $1,000 each month in health-care costs and medications. Because he's self-employed and Ellie has no coverage through her job, their health insurance has been scant and does not cover the medications for his condition.

Their debting has taken several different forms, all of which revolve around a lack of clarity, and that has left the couple more than $100,000 in debt. First, David's entrepreneurial partners have recently stopped coming up with their share of the investment payments when they're due, so David has been covering them for a year, and then not following up with the investors to collect. Second, since their medical costs are extremely high and vary significantly, they have been debting to cover them. Third, since David has been getting paid in lump sums about once every three months, the couple has been spending liberally when they get a check, and then they run out of cash before the next check arrives, using credit cards to live.

Let's take a look at the couple's first-pass Spending Plan. Note that their first Spending Plan is constructed jointly, the way they've been managing their finances, and the revised Spending Plan is split into two, with one for David and one for Ellie.

DAVID AND ELLIE'S FIRST-PASS SPENDING PLAN (JULY)

Income

July 1st paycheck	$28,332.00

Since David gets paid in a lump sum about every three months, the couple needed to allocate a little less than one-third for their monthly expenses and cover his taxes. We decided to work with $9,000 as their base for the first month, and put all other cash in a Healthy Reserve.

Income

David (Allotment for one month)	$9,000.00
Ellie	2,223.00
Total	$11,223.00

Necessities

Bills	$22,671.50
Daily Needs	3,990.00
Total	$26,661.50

Balance

$11,223.00 (income) − 26,661.50 (expenses) = $ −15,438.50

Given that David and Ellie are spending more than double their income, they're not able to save anything for the categories they identified as saving priorities.

Savings, Vacation, and Fun	**0.00**
Fun & Entertainment Money	0.00
Healthy Reserve, 3 months living expense	0.00

Short-Term Savings Account		0.00
Egypt Account		0.00
Car Repairs		0.00
Kids' College Account		0.00
Travel Account		0.00
		0.00

Monthly Plan Detail

Bills	Due	Amount
Rent	4th	1,855.00
Mortgage	15th	3,340.50
Investor payments	1st	10,000.00 (David's portion: $2,000)
Child Care (2 kids)	1st	2,000.00
Health Insurance	10th	695.00
Rx (monthly)	1st	900.00
Car 1	5th	498.00
Car 2	12th	321.00
Insurance–Car	5th	219.00
PG&E	17th	118.00
Phone, Home	18th	171.00
Blockbuster	1st	28.00
Gym	10th	295.00
Visa	3rd	390.00
Equity Credit Line	3rd	893.00
David's Student Loan	10th	398.00
Ellie's Student Loan	1st	550.00
Total		22,671.50

Daily Needs	Amount
Food	800.00
Coffee	125.00
Lunches	300.00
Fuel/Parking	350.00
Doctor Visits	1,200.00
Drug Store	30.00
Dry Cleaners	650.00

Laundry Home (coin ops)	30.00
Household	150.00
Postage	35.00
Dining out	200.00
Clothing, David	40.00
Clothing, Ellie	40.00
Clothing, Kids	40.00
Total	3,990.00

REVIEWING DAVID AND ELLIE'S FIRST-PASS PLAN

The first problem we noted about David and Ellie's method of handling their money is that they attempt to keep a joint account. I say "attempt" because having a joint account gives both of them an opportunity to be especially vague about what they have and what they can spend. In addition, since neither is clear who has the checkbook at any given time, they tend to spend without writing things down. Each has a tendency to overspend and use credit cards, and this wreaks havoc on their finances. In their first-pass Spending Plan, however, their Daily Needs were not outrageous. By taking a look at a complete list of their expenses, they were able to see that their money issues stemmed mainly from their Bills.

Once we agreed that it was important to keep separate Spending Plans—at least for Daily Needs—so that each partner can be accountable for his or her spending, we then addressed the issue of how to deal with nonregular consulting income. First and foremost, the couple had to agree to curb "Payday Debting," meaning they had to agree to put at least two-thirds of David's income in a Healthy Reserve for the months when he's not receiving a check, and then live within their means on the rest.

When we took a look at the couple's initial Spending Plan, it was obvious what was gouging their ability to remain solvent: (1) David's investor partners' defaults, which he was paying for, and (2) the couple's medical expenses. Beyond those two obvious issues, David had bought an investment home in another town that they were footing the bill for, while paying rent for the small home in which they lived. Since the market was down, they were trying to hold on to the investment property as long as possible, which seriously impacted their already fraught financial situation.

In their Daily Needs, they were overspending on groceries (storing food they couldn't really eat), dry cleaning, lunches, coffee, and household items. And they had not included amounts for estimated income taxes from David's earnings or for payments on the $40,000 owed to his parents.

REVIEWING DAVID AND ELLIE'S SECOND-PASS PLAN

After some thought and heart-to-heart discussions about what they could truly afford, David and Ellie were able to come up with reasonable changes to make their Spending Plan work. Though some of these changes felt dramatic, each choice was weighed in terms of the couple's own values. The fact that they were willing to take an honest look at what was actually happening financially—versus what they had wanted to happen—enabled them to make the changes necessary to start to live free from debt. Let's look at what they did.

DAVID AND ELLIE'S EDITED SPENDING PLANS (JULY)

Income

July 1st paycheck $28,332.00

Again, we're dividing David's income by a little less than a third, putting the balance into a Healthy Reserve account for the months he doesn't get a paycheck. Note that Bills and Daily Needs are now separated into two Spending Plans, one for David and one for Ellie, so that each is accountable for his or her portion of the family's spending. Bills and Daily Needs are divided fairly, based on each spouse's cash contributions and needs.

DAVID'S SPENDING PLAN (JULY)

Income

David (Allotment for one month) $9,000.00

Necessities

Bills	$7,378.00
Daily Needs	1,215.00
Total	$8,593.00

Balance

$9,000.00 (income) − 8,593.00 (expenses) = $407.00

Now that the couple has a balanced Spending Plan, they can each put cash aside for the things that are meaningful to them as a couple and individually.

Savings, Vacation, and Fun	**$407.00**
Fun & Entertainment Money	100.00
Healthy Reserve (joint)	50.00
Short-Term Savings Account (joint)	100.00
Car Repairs	80.00
Kids' College Account (joint)	27.00
Travel Account	50.00
Total	407.00

Note that the balance of David's large check has already been deposited into their Healthy Reserve account for the upcoming months when he won't get a check.

Monthly Plan Detail

Bills	Due	Amount	Former Amount
Rent	4th	1,855.00	
Mortgage	15th	0.00	down from 3,340.50
Investor payments	1st	0.00	down from 10,000.00
Health Insurance	1st	987.00	up from 695.00
Rx (monthly)	1st	200.00	down from 900.00
Car 1	5th	sold	down from 498.00
Car 2	12th	321.00	
Gym	10th	34.00	down from 295.00
Visa	3rd	390.00	
Equity Credit Line	3rd	893.00	

David's Student Loan	10th	398.00	
Ellie's Student Loan	1st		deferred for 6 months down from 550.00
Parents' Loan	1st	50.00	
Taxes	1st	2,250.00 (calculated at 25%)	
Total		7,378.00	

Daily Needs	Amount	Former Amount
Food	100.00	
Coffee	25.00	down from 125.00
Lunches	50.00	down from 300.00
Fuel/Parking	225.00	
Doctor Visits	300.00	down from 1,200.00
Drug Store	30.00	
Dry Cleaners	100.00	down from 650.00
Laundry Home (coin ops)	30.00	
Postage	35.00	
Dining out	200.00	
Clothing, David	60.00	up from 40.00
Clothing, Kids	60.00	up from 40.00
Total	1,215.00	

REVIEWING DAVID'S EDITED PLAN

After just one week of working their respective Debt-Free Spending Plans, David reported feeling "a mountain of stress" lift from him, since his wife was now fully sharing the financial responsibilities with him. Even though he was still responsible for the majority of the Bills based on his higher income, her full participation eased the financial pressure he felt.

The biggest decision the couple had to make was how to deal with investments that were draining their income and that they really could not afford—especially given the amount of debt they were facing. Taking an honest look at their monthly expenses, they admitted that owning a home in another town while renting where they lived didn't work for them—and when push came to shove, they really didn't want the responsibility of the investment at all.

Though they had tried to rent their investment house after the former tenants left, and then tried to sell it, the house was located in a now-devalued neighborhood, and it still sat empty after nine months. It didn't look likely that a sale was imminent. Also, since they had bought the home with an interest-only loan, they had no equity in the property. They agreed with each other to turn the property over to the bank, and to give up trying to "wait out the market." Though it wasn't an ideal choice, it was an honest one, given their financial situation.

The tougher decision was to stop pouring money into David's investment "partnership." It had become clear that the money David paid to cover his investors was unrecoverable—that, indeed, the other partners had stopped answering his calls and e-mails, and had no intention of paying David and Ellie back. David estimated that he had invested about $120,000 of leveraged money and cash in the partnership over the past year, and the projects they were funding were not doing well.

After much thought, he and Ellie agreed to relinquish their shares and walk away from the partnership, rather than pursue a legal decision. They agreed that it was a hard lesson to learn—but a valuable one. In the end, they lost a significant amount of cash in the partnership, but they gained the freedom from the stress of trying to cover those out-of-reach expenses. It was a courageous step, and not one that's for everyone, but within a year, their financial picture had improved dramatically, and they both felt lighter and better about their situation.

Let's take a look at Ellie's Spending Plan before we discuss the couple's other changes and choices.

ELLIE'S EDITED SPENDING PLAN (JULY)

Income

Ellie	$2,744.00

Note that Ellie's income has increased since their first-pass Spending Plan. When she realized what she and David's actual expenses were, she asked for a raise and got one.

Necessities

Bills	$1,378.00
Daily Needs	950.00
Total	$2,328.00

Balance

$2,744.00 (income) − 2,328.00 (expenses) = $416.00

Now that the couple has a balanced Spending Plan, they can each put cash aside for the things that are meaningful to them.

Savings, Vacation, and Fun	**$416.00**
Fun & Entertainment Money	25.00
Healthy Reserve (joint)	100.00
Short-Term Savings Account (joint)	100.00
Egypt Account	50.00
Christmas	45.00
Kids' College Account (joint)	46.00
Retirement	50.00
Total	416.00

Monthly Plan Detail

Bills	**Due**	**Amount**	**Former Amount**
Child Care	1st	1,100.00	down from 2,000.00
Car Insurance	5th	100.00	down from 219.00
PG&E	17th	79.00	down from 118.00
Phone, Home	18th	99.00	down from 171.00
Blockbuster	1st	0.00	down from 28.00
Total		1,378.00	

Daily Needs	**Amount**	**Former Amount**
Food	500.00	down from 800.00
Fuel/Parking	150.00	

Doctor Visits	50.00	down from 1,200.00
Drug Store	30.00	
Child Care	60.00	up from 0.00
Dry Cleaners	40.00	down from 650.00
Household	35.00	down from 150.00
Dining out	25.00	
Clothing, Ellie	60.00	up from 40.00
Total	950.00	

REVIEWING ELLIE'S EDITED PLAN

The first thing we note here is Ellie's increase in salary. When she and David took a realistic and detailed look at what it was costing them to live, Ellie concluded that she was being underpaid and went to her boss and asked for a raise. Her boss valued her work and agreed to pay her more. Having the evidence before her helped Ellie make the request and quelled her fears that a part-time worker might not deserve a raise. Once she asked, she felt much better about herself and what she was contributing to her family. She also requested a shift in her schedule, which meant the couple would require less child care, saving $900 a month.

Beyond the major changes in their monthly Bills listed in David's Spending Plan, there were other choices they made that helped free up cash. They bought a *more expensive* health insurance plan—an HMO that covered doctor's visits, David's meds, and preventive care—none of which were covered by their previous, high-deductible plan. That choice, by itself, saved them thousands each year. They sold one car, and David agreed to drive his parent's extra car for at least a year. Since the car was older and was no longer under warranty, David saved $80 a month in a Car Repairs Savings account, should repairs be necessary. He downsized his gym, and Ellie deferred her student loan for six months. They also created reasonable amounts for household items and groceries, and added a child-care category to Ellie's Daily Needs.

By dividing up responsibility for each area of spending, the couple also cleared up a lot of frustration about household and family duties. For instance, since Ellie liked to cook, she did most of the shopping. David kept $100 a month for convenience food, to bring home a pizza or burritos once a week to give his wife a break from preparing meals. He bought the stamps and handled trips to the post office. She took care of the children's personal-care purchases; he bought their clothes. Note that they both contribute to a Kids' College Savings account, funding this priority even though they have small children.

After a year, Ellie became pregnant again and they both agreed that David would need a corporate job to ensure the family's financial stability. He found a well-paying job at a solid tech company, and in less than a year they had paid off both of their student loans, timing the payoff with the birth of their new child.

Since their health insurance was better funded through David's job, they had more money for their monthly expenses and could add cash to their food, entertainment, and household categories. They used his bonuses as windfall money, stashing one-third for kids' child care, preschool, and lessons; one-third to pay off debt; and one-third for fun. And, because they had clarity with their new Debt-Free Spending Plans, they were able to fund a year off work for Ellie to be at home with the new baby—without debt.

Note that when they started their Spending Plans, both David and Ellie had avoidance problems regarding paying bills, keeping a checkbook register, balancing costs against income, and keeping track of debt. They were both overspenders and credit card debtors. Since both had trouble, they agreed to make each partner responsible for *some* Bills and *some* Daily Needs. That meant having separate Spending Plans and assigning some of the responsibilities for family needs to each of them.

This agreement solved more than their money issues. It helped them solve the issue of fair division of labor in the family, and it stopped resentments and fights over who was working harder. Each partner contributed what he or she agreed to, and that created peace in their home. In fact, both David and Ellie found themselves regularly thanking the other for his or her contributions to the family. That spirit of generosity and appreciation enhanced their marriage and brought the laughter back into their home.

10

. . . . .

Keeping on Track and Keeping It Real
Using the Tools That Help You Stay on the Plan

THE MOST POWERFUL tool in our new debt-free life is obviously our Debt-Free Spending Plan. This is the centerpiece that makes everything else work. The reason we could never live within our means before is that we lived in vagueness about our money and we never had a plan to guide us in our spending. Now, we do. Every month of every year—for the rest of our lives—we will know what we have to live on, and we will know what we have to spend. We're never, ever, going to put money into our account and wing it again. And if we take that little bit of time each month to edit and tweak, and use our Debt-Free Spending Plan, we will always, always stay sane and free concerning our money. That's a promise.

So, beyond the tools discussed so far, what else is there to help us? What else do we need to know?

There are plenty of tools to help keep us solidly on the path of a debt-free life. These tools fall into three categories: (1) tech tools, (2) bottom-line tools, and (3) coaching and support tools. Let's take a look at each in turn.

Tech Tools

Tech tools are exactly what they sound like—technological toys that can help us in our debt-free life.

At the beginning of this book I promised that you would not have to learn any new software in order to master the Debt-Free Spending Plan. And that's why, throughout this book, I've provided information and tips in simple lists. *Why is that important?* Because most of us debtors freak out, shut down, and go blank when it comes to figures and finances—and that's part of the reason we got into the money mess we've found ourselves in. We can't *hear* when it comes to numbers.

So anything that requires learning a new technical skill in order to live debt-free is going to be a road block. Even though we're more than smart enough to figure out how to use these tech tools, when it comes to money, most of us crumble—we lose the ability to compute or comprehend even the basics of addition and subtraction. In other words, we first need to learn how to use the Debt-Free Spending Plan in its most basic form; then, once we've got that down pat, we can make it work using any tech tool that we choose. And, of course, we can choose not to use tech tools at all, too.

It's not that we're not *bright* enough to figure out Quicken, Quickbooks, or the latest financial smartphone app. It's not that we *can't* figure out how to link financial programs to our checking account balance. Our challenge is that, with a new skill to learn, we will almost always create a "block" to learning the tech skill as an avoidance technique for dealing with our finances. Can I tell you how many debtors I've worked with who can manage intricate databases and software programs at work, but who *lose it* when trying to learn Quicken for their own finances? Can I tell you how many people I know who manage mega-budgets at their jobs, but who shut down on the addition and subtraction that shows that their expenses are greater than their income? That's why I have explained the Debt-Free Spending Plan in simple lists.

That said, the world has changed and we're in the smartphone era. Most of us have gained some technological savvy, and many of us really enjoy it. So for those of you who love the world of new technology and what it offers, there are tools galore. If a tool enhances your ability to live debt-free, then use it. If it's just another duty-bound, busy-item to learn, then skip it. Remember that you can do all of this work on a simple Word document, in an Excel spreadsheet, or on a sheet of paper. It doesn't matter.

So, for those of you who are comfortable in the tech world, what's available?

SMARTPHONE APPS

There are dozens of financial apps that are iPhone and smartphone compatible, which can make your financial tracking accessible wherever you are. Type in "smartphone financial apps" in Google or another search engine, and you'll get a nice long list and plenty of reviews. About.com offers terrific reviews and information on Mint, SplashMoney, Google Wallet, Ultrasoft Money, and more. Some, like Ultrasoft Money, offer an option to reallocate money if you go over your budget categories—much like our Magic Little Notebook format—and that function is particularly useful and even necessary sometimes. (The Magic Notebook, you remember, is based on the ability to move money from, say, postage to dry cleaning, if you need a little extra in one category.)

If you love these mobile programs, by all means, use them. Having a notebook-type app in your phone is a terrific feature. It lets you download all of your entered expenses to your laptop when the month is over, meaning you don't have to enter the information twice (once in your notebook, and once again in your tracking record). But here's the thing—don't think that because you're tracking your expenses with some cool, new toy that you can skip the *planning* part of the Debt-Free Spending Plan. In other words, some apps and programs will offer you budgeting tools that you can use to plan your monthly expenses, compatibly with the Debt-Free Spending Plan format, but others won't.

Remember what we agreed to in Chapter 2? We don't spend one damn dime until we have created our Debt-Free Spending Plan. It does absolutely no good to keep track of what you're spending without a *plan* for how *much* to spend in each Daily Needs category. So don't even dream that applying some groovy tech app is going to absolve you of needing to work out your Spending Plan each month.

Use technology or don't—it's up to you. But if you want to stay sane and debt-free with your money, your Debt-Free Spending Plan—even written down on paper—takes priority over tracking tools, every single time.

INTERNET BANKING

First and foremost, Internet banking is, for most of us, a gift. We get a user ID and a password from our bank, and we can access our accounts online any time of the day. We can link our checking accounts to our savings accounts, and we can move money from one account to the other, effortlessly. This is particularly useful if we're using multiple savings accounts, as recommended in Chapter 4.

We can deposit our checks into our checking accounts or Healthy Reserve, and simply divvy up the savings money online at our own convenience. Most of us are already using this tool. If you're not, and you need an explanation, go into your bank or call them and let them walk you through the setup process.

INTERNET SAVINGS ACCOUNTS

The most popular savings account systems among my clients are the ones offered by online banks such as ING Direct or Emigrant Direct. These Internet banking services offer users an unlimited number of savings accounts; you name them, deposit funds in them, and can easily move money back into a checking account when it's time to use them. The ING Direct and Emigrant savings accounts pay a decent interest rate without fees or minimum balances. (There are many such services. Check online to find the online bank that best serves your needs.) The slight disadvantage is that it can take a day or two for money to move from an Internet account to your checking account, but that's also an advantage. The transfer time means you have to think ahead about the money move, and it's more likely that you will use your savings in accordance with your Debt-Free Spending Plan and your goals. (See www.ingdirect.com for more details.) There are plenty of similar financial savings tools available to help you save, so if you choose to use them, check out their capabilities online first and choose the one that's best for you.

MULTIPLE SAVINGS ACCOUNTS AT YOUR BANK

You can open multiple savings accounts at your bank the same way as you can with ING Direct or Emigrant accounts or other Internet savings plans, but at some banks there is a service charge for these accounts. However, at Wells Fargo and similar banks, you can create an automatic deposit from your checking account of at least $25 a month, and the savings account service charge is waived. Ask about this feature when you open any accounts, as a customer service representative may not offer free accounts unless you ask for them.

At some banks, there is no service charge for maintaining savings accounts as long as one account has a minimum balance in it. The general rule of thumb for all debtors is: Get clarity before you open any accounts. No "surprises" of $50 in unanticipated service charges. Also, note that many banks place limits on the number of monthly savings account transactions allowed unless you physically go into the bank. (The limit is usually three or four per month.)

CREDIT UNIONS

Don't forget about credit unions when choosing a financial institution to bank with. Many offer free checking accounts, higher interest rates, and cheaper secured loans for cars and homes. They are also most often community-based institutions that have not invested in derivatives or other risky investments. A credit union will usually allow liberal use of various ATMs as well, making them a good choice all around. But get clarity before you sign up. Know the terms, know the benefits, and ask questions.

BANK-SPONSORED SPENDING PLANS

Many banks are now offering what they call "spending plans." They are, more accurately, spending *records* with some savings goals noted. Though these may be helpful for others, they are not comprehensive enough for us debtors. Remember that *tracking* is not the same as *planning*, and tracking alone will not get you where you need to be. So make sure that whatever you're using to implement your Debt-Free Spending Plan incorporates all of the principles in this book. Those five items are:

1. A monthly Spending Plan for how to pay Bills and allot Daily Needs

2. A daily record keeper like the Magic Little Notebook that keeps you on track

3. A Bill-Paying Plan that assigns specific Bills to specific pay-checks

4. Separate savings accounts based on what's meaningful to you

5. A record of what was spent where

Most banking software is not sophisticated enough to cover all of these planning areas, so don't opt out of a usable Debt-Free Spending Plan for a tool that is not going to get at the heart of your debting issues.

PERSONAL FINANCIAL APPS AND THE DEBT-FREE SPENDING PLAN

As noted above, there are handfuls of financial apps ready and able to serve you. Search the Net for your favorites, and use whatever works. Just make sure that what you use covers the five imperative-for-debtors capabilities listed above. If an app does not cover one or more of these five imperative areas, don't even kid yourself that you can use it to stay solvent. You're better off making a list on paper than using a tech app that doesn't help you plan your spending. Only use what *actually* will work for a debtor—that is, explicitly clear coverage of everything you need to stay solvent.

I'll say it one more time. A working Debt-Free Spending Plan includes: (1) planning for monthly Bills and Daily Needs totals, (2) a running total of Daily Needs spending in the form of a Magic Little Notebook (so you know, as you go, how much you have left to spend), (3) a Bill-Paying Plan that allocates cash based on when you get paid, (4) savings accounts for what you want and need, and (5) a record of all of it. Got it?

In that vein, Mint.com, Pocket Money (catamount.com), SplashMoney (Splashdata.com), Day Bank (quantumquinn.com), or Pennies (designbyaknife.com) all have easy-to-use formats and are either free or inexpensive to download. If they add to your debt-free living experience and you like them, then use them. Some apps will have planning ability; some will not. Remember, planning and Daily Needs management are always going to take precedent over a tracking-only approach to your finances.

When we plan first, and then live within our Spending Plans, we always stay out of debt.

Bottom-Line Tools

Many of us, when we begin to learn how to live debt-free, have been ignoring the bottom-line tools that might help us get clarity with our end-of-the-month numbers. We don't balance our checkbooks, and we don't track our expenditures, so we have no clear idea of where our money was spent. Oftentimes, we never learned how to use these tools. So, though it may seem basic for those who already know how, we're going to take a few moments and explain how these tools work.

Remember that it's extremely helpful to balance your checkbook and keep track of what you spend, but even if all you do each month is create a Debt-Free Spending Plan and live by it, using your Magic Little Notebook, you will always stay solvent. The reason I recommend using bottom-line tools is simple: Sometimes, in daily life, you'll forget to write an entry in your Magic Little Notebook, and your bank statement will reveal that. You may also need to track end-of-the-year expenditures for your business or your taxes. So, having a system that gives you a balance at the end of the month is just a good idea. Let's review some tools that can help you do that.

QUICKEN AND QUICKBOOKS FOR YOUR RECORD KEEPING

The most popular of the personal accounting and small business software packages are Quicken and Quickbooks. Both are powerful tools that can be set up in accordance with the personal Debt-Free Spending Plan categories. Both will give monthly totals, year-end totals, and reports, and both can interact with your bank accounts.

Both offer the ability to check off bank expenses (those that show up on your bank statement) against your Quicken or Quickbooks categories. If you love Quicken, Quickbooks, or a similar tool, then feel free to set up your Debt-Free Spending Plan categories inside it. Just remember that you still have to plan your expenses each month. Once again, tracking expenditures after you've spent the money is never enough.

If you don't know how to use either of these programs, try working your Spending Plan in a simple list first (on a Word document, in Excel, or even by hand on graph paper) and learn a financial program later. Though it will seem rudimentary at the beginning, the simplicity will appeal to the 10-year-old in you who shuts down around numbers and money math.

There's one major danger for debtors using these software tracking programs. Let's say you learn Quicken and you get all excited about your success with it, and so you set up as many categories and subcategories of Bills and Daily Needs as you can think of. You feel really smart and organized—maybe even thrilled that you're so *together*. But what happens next month, or three months from now, once the novelty has worn off?

This is what happens: We take a look at our Quicken setup, and it's so detailed and burdensome in its exquisitely divided and subdivided categories that—you guessed it!—we tune out on it and stop focusing on our finances altogether. It is our objective—no matter what tool we're using—to keep it simple. Remember? No more than ten or twelve categories for Daily Needs. In other words, you want to create categories that are specific enough to be useful and still broad enough that you're not tracking endless detail. For instance, it's just not useful to track endless subcategories under the food category (e.g., meat, fish, produce, dairy, lunches, snacks, take-out, etc.). Trust me: If you subdivide in that much detail, you will very shortly lose your mind and your will to work your Spending Plan.

No matter what tools we're using, we watch out for this pitfall and we *always keep it simple*.

BANK STATEMENTS AND BALANCING YOUR ACCOUNTS

We have yet to discuss the balancing of monthly bank statements in this book. How come? Because debtors tend to get overwhelmed with too much math—even when we're good at it in other arenas of our lives. So many debtors brag that they "haven't balanced a bank statement in twenty years," that it's almost a cliché. *Why should we care if we balance our bank statement?* Truly, if we know how much money we have to spend in our accounts, and we live within those amounts by using our Debt-Free Spending Plans, why would we ever need to balance the damned thing?

And the answer is simple: Because we're human and we make mistakes. Here's what we should be doing. We should be entering our purchases in our Magic Little Notebooks *and* our checking account registers. The registers will give us what's *actually* in our accounts, and our Magic Little Notebook will balance what we should be spending in each Daily Needs category against our Spending Plan. If we forget to enter items in our Magic Little Notebook for one or two days, we just pick up where we left off and enter our receipts the next day. No big deal. But we don't want to stray from that notebook for long. It's our Magic Little Notebook that's going to keep us solvent, so that's the most important entry.

So why should we enter stuff in our check registers at all? Because we need a balancing point, a checklist at the end of the month of what we actually spent versus what we recorded. We're human, so we just forget sometimes. That's part of the game.

Things happen. It's raining, and we jump in the car and forget to enter a fuel purchase. We run from the grocery store to pick up the kids, and we forget to enter the food totals. We go on a mental vacation while we're delivering a big project at work, and we forget all about two days of expenses. That's just normal human stuff. So we do our bank statements at the end of the month to balance all of that out. We don't sweat it, and we don't panic. We just balance it.

Since most of us debtors have never balanced a checkbook before, let's take a moment to understand the basic premise. It's a simple list with some addition and subtraction. If you can do the Debt-Free Spending Plan, you can balance a checkbook.

The balance on the bank statement usually throws us because it's not current. It's days behind our monthly spending, and it covers stuff we've long forgotten about. We may also check our online transactions during the month, and that might mentally trip us up about where we really are and what's been accounted for. Here's my advice: Balance your checkbook once a month, when your paper or online statement comes, and don't do it in between. *Why?* Because you'll drive yourself crazy trying to balance and rebalance the same items. Simplify your life, and trust that your Spending Plan is working for you. As long as you live within your plan, you won't go over.

So, here's how balancing a checkbook works:

1. Take out your checkbook register and match each item to those listed on your monthly bank statement. Note that everything on your statement will be out of order because the stores you bought from submit their charges at various times. Be patient while you find the matching checks and debit card items on your statement.

Always match the checkbook register to the statement—meaning that you go in order, noting each item from your register first, then matching it to your statement. If you notice that you missed something—say, a Trader Joe's expense of 35.99 shows up on your bank statement and you don't have it in your check register—then write it in your checkbook.

Here's how you make that addition to your check register: Use a few lines in your register below your last entry, and write "adjustments" in there. Then list all of the entries you missed during the month, with a positive or negative symbol next to them. It looks like this:

CHECKBOOK REGISTER— REGULAR ENTRIES AND "ADJUSTMENTS"

				$1,303.11
7/4	Debit	Eagle Gas		36.98
				1,266.13
7/5	Check #3356	PG&E		89.17
				$1,176.96

Adjustments

6/15	Debit	Trader Joe's	−35.99	
6/18	Debit	Postage	−8.13	
6/20	Deposit	Target-return	+12.33	
	Adjustment balance			−31.79
				$1,145.17

Once you've checked off all of the items in your check register against your bank statement, and have made your adjustments for what you forgot to write down, you use this adjusted amount to balance against the bank's numbers. In this example, the new number for the checkbook balance is $1,145.17. Put another way, this is what *you* say you have. Now let's see what the *bank* says you have.

2. How do you figure out what the *bank* says you have? And how do you do that, given that you've been spending for a good week or more since the bank's cut-off date on your statement? The balancing act is a simple add-and-subtract list.

Find the *account balance* listed on the top of your bank statement, and write it on the top line of a worksheet. (Usually worksheets come enclosed with your paper statement. If you don't get one, just follow the format below—it's easy.) Note the date the statement was sent— say, July 17, for our example. Then write in any deposits that weren't on your statement—in other words, you're going to list *deposits* that you made after the bank statement cut-off date. Then list whatever you *spent* (debit or check) after the statement cut-off date—it'll be a good list of stuff. It looks like this:

BANK BALANCE WORKSHEET

Bank balance says: 569.17

My deposits (new ones not noted on statement)

+1,633.12 (paycheck)
+23.14 (Kohl's return)
Subtotal 1,656.26

My debits/checks/withdrawals not noted on statement

−16.33 Walgreens
−35.22 Dean's Market
−30.11 Eagle Gas
−101.91 AT&T
−68.99 Verizon
−394.00 Blue Shield
−429.00 Chase car payment
−12.99 A-1 Cleaners
−4.64 Barrone Café
−2.13 Peet's Coffee
−6.78 Mollie Stone's Market
Subtotal 1,102.10

Now, add the bank balance ($569.17) to your new deposits. Your new deposits total in this example is $1,656.26. Then subtract the new debits and checks. It looks like this:

Bank Balance on Statement	569.17
Deposits: Add new deposits to the bank balance*	+1,656.26
Subtotal	+2,225.43
Debits: Subtract the new debits/expenses*	−1,102.10
Total	1,123.33

*These are new deposits and debits—items that haven't shown up on your bank statement yet.

3. Now, you balance the amount from your bank statement worksheet against what you have written in your check register. Your checkbook balance was 1,145.17. The bank says you have about $20 less than you think you have.

1,145.17	This is what you say you have
−1,123.33	This is what your bank statement balance worksheet says you have
−21.84	Your difference

Note that if you use a software program to balance your bank statement, you'll simply check off debits and deposits inside the program. Quicken (or whatever you're using) will link with your checking account, dump all of your bank activity into it, and you'll do your balancing inside the program. But *don't* wait until you learn how to do this to balance your bank statement.

In fact, for us debtors it's often better to learn how to do the balancing on paper so that we understand the principles involved. Most of us have never, ever balanced a statement, so we want to make it as easy for ourselves as possible by just learning the procedure on paper first.

■　■　■

If, after all the efforts you've made in the month to balance your money, you're still a little off—say $20 or so, as in the example above—*just write it off.* Decide what your comfort level is for these tiny adjustments, and call it even. If you can afford to float an error of $20 or $50 or $100 without pain, then don't spend nine hours trying to find the error to balance your statement to the penny. You can if you really want to, but remember the principle that prevents us all from losing our minds with this financial stuff. That is, *we just have clarity for today.*

DON'T SWEAT THE SMALL STUFF

In my own Debt-Free Spending Plan, I can afford to adjust $20, or even $50, but if I'm off by $100 or more, then I do need to do some research to figure out what I missed. More and more, though, because I use my Spending Plan so diligently, my errors in balancing my bank statement are so small that I just say *Who cares?* I make the $21.84 adjustment, and move on. So, just decide what your comfort level is when you're balancing your checkbook, and live there, without killing yourself.

THE ENVELOPE STASH METHOD

This is a simple tool I employ to keep from depriving myself of important items. When I began using my Debt-Free Spending Plan, I had a compulsion to usurp any clothing money I had allotted in order to pay off debt. I felt I didn't "deserve" clothing money because I owed my creditors. I also knew that later, after using the money for debt payments, I'd feel angry, and I would want to act out and use my credit cards again for clothes. Since I had stopped debting, that viscious cycle wasn't an option. I *had* to employ a new tool.

So I developed the "envelope stash method." It's simple. Whatever I tended to deprive myself of got taken out of my bank account in cash and put into an envelope clearly labeled for that purpose. For example, some of my stash envelopes were designated for haircut, entertainment, clothes, and art supplies. Once I put the cash in the envelopes, I wasn't allowed to use it for any other purpose. I couldn't take it out of my checking account for something else (since it was already out), and I couldn't usurp it to pay some other bill. When I shopped for clothes or art supplies, I'd bring my envelope and pay cash. I didn't shop for that item without the envelope.

My haircuts are a terrific example of how the envelope stash method can work with regular but nonmonthly expenses. I get a haircut once every three months ($144 with tip), and I will, if left to my own devices, "forget" to plan for this expense. So I put $48 a month in the "haircut" envelope, and when there's $144 in it, I know it's time to make an appointment. I always have haircut money, never deprive myself in that area of self-care, and never gouge my Spending Plan with an unplanned $144 expense. It's always planned for, always set aside.

Now that I trust myself more with my Spending Plan, I can keep my art supplies and clothing money in my account, and I know that I won't cheat myself by spending it on something else. Part of our work with the Debt-Free Spending Plan is to learn to trust it—that if we follow the plan, we will have money for *everything* we need. Once we get that confidence, we will relax; but until then, we do whatever we can to ensure that we keep the money we have set aside for the things we need and love.

Coaching and Other Support Tools

Many of us have been in debt for so many years that the very thought of dealing with our money troubles makes us check out altogether. But not being able to face our money challenges does not mean we should keep ignoring them. What it does mean is that we may need some help getting to the starting line, or we may need a hand getting over the few first hurdles of addressing our debt issues. This doesn't mean we're weak or that there's something wrong with us; it just means we need a little support in dealing with what's difficult.

So, if you've read this far in this book, and you're still panicky, it's probably a good idea to think about getting some extra help. Some forms of help cost money—which can be problematic when you're still debting—and some of it is free. Please use whatever works for you. Getting some extra help can make a life-changing difference in your willingness to work the Debt-Free Spending Plan.

PERSONAL COACHING

Because so many of us have had trouble with our money, and because we often shut down when it comes to finances, it might be wise to invest in some personal coaching on debt-free living. Look for a counselor who can help support you specifically in setting up your Debt-Free Spending Plan. Our object is not to discuss our past behavior; our goal is to get direct support to *change* our behavior. The way I structure my own counseling is simple: I spend three to four hours with a client (or a couple) setting up a personal Debt-Free Spending Plan (or, in the case of a couple, two plans), and then we meet by phone for three 45-minute sessions each month.

Usually, my clients have mastered the basics of the Debt-Free Spending Plan after about three months of using it and tweaking it. Some of my clients have used coaching for longer periods to get monthly support in handling variable income levels, or to help in building a small business in a debt-free way, or just because they like the comfort that the counseling offers. Some have said that the counseling makes a difference in their ability to keep focused on living debt-free. Several clients check in with me as needed when they have life changes that affect their money.

It doesn't matter how you structure the counseling, but if you need help and support to get debt-free, please don't sit on the fence. Obtain what you need to fix what's broken. Look at it this way: If your car is clunking along the freeway, you wouldn't hesitate to take it to the mechanic. When the questions are financial, there are a million ways to find the help you need—it's not limited to one way. But the Debt-Free Spending Plan, as described in this book, is designed specifically for us debtors, so please—apply it as much as you can, however you can. The book is here to help, the principles are here to help, and I'm here to help, if you so choose.

DEBTORS ANONYMOUS

Certainly, as I said above, there are a million ways to find health and wholeness, and a support program is just one of them. But here's what I know: If you cannot stop using credit cards or borrowing money, then you need support. *Find something that can support you.* Debtors Anonymous is free, it's nonsectarian, it's anonymous, and it has no creed or "right way" to get solvent. There are in-person meetings in towns and cities across the country (and the world) and phone meetings available at set times for anyone who's interested. (You can find local meetings and phone meetings at http://www.debtors anonymous.org.)

The advantage of the group setting is the sharing of individual, real stories, so that you hear how others have solved dilemmas similar to your own. The group setting is a leveling of individuals—regardless of background or education or income, everyone in the group stops feeling alone and gets support from the others for keeping their numbers in the black and for living debt-free. It's hugely valuable, and just going to *listen* can change your life. If you need the support, go get it. It's free and it's there for you. There are dozens of other no-cost community and online support groups to help you as well. Look up "debt support groups" in any search engine or phone book to find one that works for you.

No Excuses

You now know that there are no excuses left to keep on debting. Debt is painful. It's bad for you, your family, your well-being, your ability to make choices in your life, and your future. So don't wait another minute. The tools are here for you.

If you're willing to write a long-hand Debt-Free Spending Plan on graph paper and keep a Magic Little Notebook, *use it* and you will get better. If you're into all things technological and you want to set up the Bills and Daily Needs figures in any one of dozens of financial apps, *use it* and you will recover from debting.

It doesn't matter how sophisticated you are or how many tools you employ. If you begin, right now, you will get relief. If you use the Debt-Free Spending Plan, employing it every day and every month—you will get well. You will no longer go into debt, you will no longer stress about money, and you will no longer feel badly about yourself and your finances. *You'll get free.*

You will have peace with your money for probably the first time in your life. It's incredible to contemplate, but I guarantee you: If you follow this simple plan, you absolutely, positively will.

11

. . . . .

To File or Not to File
Bankruptcy and Our
Future Financial Health

FILING FOR bankruptcy is a serious step, one that brings with it some long-term ramifications. So, it's a decision we debtors must consider carefully, and then consider again. In this chapter, my goal is to deal primarily with the decision of whether to file or not.

Do I File for Bankruptcy?
The first thing to know about bankruptcy is this: *It is institutionalized debt forgiveness*. In other words, our culture acknowledges that sometimes people need an "out " when they have made the huge mistake of large-scale debting and there's no other solution. For example, did

you have a costly divorce settlement and now you're making less than half of what you used to make? Did you go into debt to cover expensive medical bills and now you can't pay those bills? Maybe you dropped the homeowner's insurance, then lost the house in a fire, and now you can't sell the property. Maybe you ran up debts for a small business that tanked, or went out of control with personal debting and now need to turn your life around. These are all scenarios that we can fall into financially as debtors, and—God bless us—our country recognizes the need for an escape hatch.

So the first thing those of us contemplating bankruptcy need to ask ourselves is: *Do we have large-scale debt?* Large-scale debt is debt that is so huge in relation to our income or our profession that it is *unreasonable* to think that we will ever be able to pay it back. It is debt for which the monthly minimum payments are so high that we cannot pay and still reasonably fund our living expenses. It is debt that is so debilitating that it will crush us unless there's relief.

That said, several of my clients have chosen to continue to pay small amounts toward debts of over $100,000, even when they have incomes that are less than half of their debts. This is an individual decision to make. But if your debt is so large that you cannot reasonably pay the minimums each month, or the debt already—before penalties—outweighs your living-expense income by a large percentage, then bankruptcy may be a reasonable option.

Remember: We do have the choice to pay whatever we can—say, even $5 a month on each debt, accompanied by a letter about our financial circumstances. But if we continue to pay less than our minimums, the balances will eventually go to a collection agency, and our credit ratings will be dinged anyway. This is why many people, when faced with this reality, consider bankruptcy.

Because of its popularity in the last decade, bankruptcy has become a bit harder to declare than it used to be. There are more steps involved and it costs a bit more than it used to. But it's still relatively affordable in relation to large-scale debt.

Attorneys and Agencies

The first question, once you decide that bankruptcy is an option, is how to pay the lawyer or service firm. Remember, you do not want to debt anymore, not even for a bankruptcy attorney. There are numerous services and agencies that can help those of us who need bankruptcy assistance. So, if you need those services and assistance, Google "free bankruptcy services" or "low-cost, nonprofit bankruptcy services" and your city's name, and you will locate some help. (Beware of scams and hype, however; check out all attorneys, firms, and agencies first on "Yelp," or contact the Better Business Bureau [www.bbb.org], or use other review services, such as state-run supervisory agencies. The best reference for a bankruptcy attorney is a personal one.)

If you are going to proceed with bankruptcy, keep all your records, both credit and income related, and all letters you've sent to creditors. For example, if you've been sending $5 or $10 a month on large debts, make sure to send those payments with a letter and keep a copy of those letters to send to your attorney. Also, always get three contrasting quotes on any major services you pay for, including bankruptcy attorneys.

Ethical Issues

There are ethical issues related to bankruptcy, which we need to consider. For example, how do we determine if we can accept this form of debt forgiveness?

The criterion we use to determine whether we can accept bankruptcy as an option is the same criterion we use for debt forgiveness from any other source: *We don't accept debt forgiveness unless we are truly living debt-free.* It's just as if parents or friends have loaned us money and offer to forgive the debt. We don't accept the debt forgiveness offered in bankruptcy unless we have changed our behavior regarding our money. And that means we have been following a

Debt-Free Spending Plan; we've become proficient at it, and we work it as best we can. We do not use credit cards, take out loans, or do any personal borrowing of any other kind. And we know clearly what it costs us to live each month, and we fund those expenses debt-free.

If this is our new lifestyle and our new commitment, and we truly cannot pay back the debt, then we have the integrity to ask for debt forgiveness.

Be Honest

In filling out the bankruptcy forms, we tell the truth. We don't dodge, duck, or cover. We say what happened, without blame or shame. That is, we say that we borrowed more than we could reasonably pay, we got caught up in debting, and we lacked clarity on how we would pay back the money. We lived beyond our means, without clear numbers on what it costs us to live. And, we state that we have changed that behavior.

In any bankruptcy process, we will be asked to list our monthly expenses. Since we already have a Debt-Free Spending Plan, all of that work is done. We also write a statement, in some part of our request for debt relief, that states that we are working a Debt-Free Spending Plan, that we get support (if we do), and that we are committed to living debt-free for the rest of our lives. If our apology is made real in our changed behavior, then it makes sense to tell the bankruptcy court how our behavior has changed.

The Fallout of Filing

So what will happen to our credit ratings if we decide to file for bankruptcy? If the state decides to approve a request for debt relief in the form of bankruptcy, all three credit agencies will report that the debts have been discharged—meaning that they were unpaid and were settled to a zero balance.

Those credit records will affect us in several different ways. First, unpaid, settled balances will remain on the credit record for seven years. Second, we will not be able to apply for regular-interest home loans or many other kinds of loans for a period of time, most often at least four years. Third, we will not be able to apply for new lines of credit for a period of time. Since we do not debt or use credit cards anymore, these timelines are of little concern to us.

The Devil in Disguise

Note that, since we're living debt-free, we are unconcerned about applying for large or small lines of credit. We no longer use those sources, and we no longer need them. We may, however, be concerned about buying a house or a car—these are secured loans, the only kind of loan we now consider. After bankruptcy, we acknowledge that there needs to be a period of time when we live debt-free before that can become a possibility. Some lenders may charge extreme high-interest rates to lure us into a loan more quickly. Stay out of that racket. It's just a different kind of debt, and it is predatory lending.

Don't be surprised if a few months after your final bankruptcy approval, you receive dozens of new offers for credit cards. Creditors often target the newly bankrupted, offering "credit repair" deals. Rip them up as soon as they arrive. Even some self-help books and credit-repair advisers will tell debtors to get right back on the "debting horse," suggesting that they get a credit card of any kind to begin "rebuilding" their credit. *Do not fall for this nonsense.*

I've worked with many debtors who have filed for bankruptcy, only to start the whole debting cycle all over again with a new set of credit cards and credit lines. *We do not debt again.* Period. We certainly don't disparage the people and institutions who have had faith in us—faith that we have broken by filing for bankruptcy and not paying our balances—by debting again with a new set of creditors. The likelihood that we'll have debt trouble again is huge.

We recognize that debting is a *compulsion*, like drinking too much, and we stay out of the bar.

If we choose to save for a house, then we might have to save more money than the average person would in order to qualify for a loan. So be it. We do not debt for anything—ever again. That's how our financial life works for us from now on. When we abide by this simple debt-free approach, we will always stay free of money stress and all of its attendant ills. We did not work this hard to learn how to live debt-free just to climb down into the hellish hole of debting again. So we stay *out*.

12

. . . . .

Building a Life of Financial Integrity

THE DEFINITION of the word *integrity* is: "Soundness of moral principle and character; uprightness; honesty; state of being whole, entire, or undiminished; sound; unimpaired. See honor." That definition describes exactly what we're after in our financial lives. We want a sound foundation for our spending—one that is based on solid character and the good choices that go with that. We want to be upright in our dealings with our money. We want to be honest about the things that are important to us, and we want to fund them, no matter how small the amounts we begin with.

We want to be whole in our approach to money and living, meaning that we fund more than just our bills and expenses. We also fund our vacations, entertainment, special projects, and big financial goals because those are what make for a happy, whole, and fulfilled life. We live committed to the process of living debt-free—which means we live lives that are undiminished by money stress and money drama.

We are sound in our approach to all things financial, and our lives take on a solidness of purpose: a clarity of direction and a daily, working knowledge of what's important to us. We are unimpaired in our ability to express our gifts in the world, and we direct our solvent ship toward the things that we want to experience. We are all about what's meaningful to us, and we fund the path that leads in that direction every day, with honor.

That's the crux of the whole idea behind the Debt-Free Spending Plan: We have been living without honor, but now, because we live debt-free, our path is full of honor. We know what we have to live on, and we live within our means. We spend based on our values, and we live by them. Our relationships with others improve. We can focus on our work. We are better partners, better parents, and better friends. We know what moves our souls. We are clear, strong, and vividly alive in our worlds. We are honorable. We are—mercifully and finally—living with integrity, living in peace with our money.

Success Is Going to Look Different Now

I began this book with the tale of my disastrous debting and the awful effects it had on my life. I was sick—emotionally, physically, and financially. My relationships and my work life were a mess. I had hives, nightmares, and insomnia. I was out of work, out of cash and credit, and out of options. And to those truly amazing people who sat me down and gave me the first tools of living debt-free, bless you. You know who you are and you saved my life.

I created the Debt-Free Spending Plan out of what I learned, and what I knew I needed. And by now, I've shared it with many, many individuals and couples who've also learned to create peace in their lives by using it. It has, for me, for my marriage, and for those I've worked with, been a miracle. I am proud every day of the debt-free life I live and how that has translated into giving help and hope to other debtors.

But working the Debt-Free Spending Plan has altered me in another way, too. My experience of success has changed. In fact, it has been revolutionized. I've known a lot of successful people in my life, and I've often felt marginalized by their monetary accomplishments— certainly by what I assumed was their luck, and even sometimes, by their privilege. But many of these successful people have said the same thing: "Jo, it's not about the money." That always seemed like so much whitewashing to me, especially from the vantage point of not having reached that success myself. And certainly in support groups, I witnessed people with wild amounts of money who were still in debt. So I did learn that debting is a process addiction, and it doesn't have anything to do with actual amounts of cash. But since learning to live debt-free, I've discovered what success really is—what "succeeding" means, in the best sense. It's about more than making money or having money.

In working the Debt-Free Spending Plan I have stumbled upon my own, new version of success, and I find it so much more powerful and fulfilling and true. I have found out that success is the ability to make the choices I want to make and to be able to fund them. Oddly enough, it turns out for me, succeeding has turned out to be reliant much more on the clarity of debt-free choices than it is about large amounts of cash.

Success, for me, looks like this: I write, I paint, I make music, I practice yoga and teach it, I work on environmental causes, I help people get well financially. I'm no longer tied to a job I hate, and I'm no longer cycling through jobs I can barely tolerate. I fund all of these aspects of myself, as well as my desire to share these gifts. Since I do everything debt-free and I have savings as well, my creative projects have a nice, long growth period to bloom into something viable. My life has started to take the shape of my interests, and that means I own it and I like it. My relationships have improved and my marriage works.

Yes, there are still problems, angsty decisions, and stuff that comes up out of nowhere to throw a monkey wrench in the works. But because I live debt-free, I'm clear about which way to turn, which boundaries to set, and what's out of balance. In other words, my path is my own now. But none of that would have taken place if I had not learned to live debt-free.

It's bigger than the years I made big money. It's bigger than wishing someone would come along and "save" me. It's bigger than the dreams of grandeur, and certainly it's bigger than all of the trouble, the dead-ends, the panic, and the angst of debting. Living debt-free has given me genuine, heart-felt choices in my life, which has been invaluable to my happiness.

The Real Jackpot

Your new debt-free life will revolutionize how you move in the world. It will take you out of the credit maze and will give you the ultimate gift of living: clarity.

The Debt-Free Spending Plan certainly gives you the precise information to plan for what you need to live on, and it offers you the daily tools to manage your money. But as you work it, you will find that, over time, it also gives you choices about much more. It's both an importance barometer and a call to action, guiding you to turn your attention, time, and cash toward what you love. It will help you fund the things you need to feed your soul. And that, at the end of the day, is the true jackpot. That is the kind of success that lands you at your ninetieth birthday with no regrets.

The Happy Life

As we practice living a debt-free life, there is a shift that occurs inside us, a fundamental change in how we live. Clarity guides our choices and our actions, and we live free from money stress. Even though it takes a small amount of effort to maintain our numbers and enter our receipts, when we do so, we feel an immediate sense of ease. Even if we drop the ball every now and then, we still have a structure—and we can put ourselves right back on track, with our eyes on clarity. We feel, *Yes, I'm alright.*

We can put the worries that we don't know where our money is going to rest, and we can focus on other things. With our financial worries set aside, we begin—slowly and subtly, and then clearly and decisively—to direct our lives toward what we really want to accomplish. When we give ourselves over to what we want to experience, fully funded by our debt-free spending and our own ingenuity, we're happier. We're steadier. We're easier to be with. We're more fun. We have integrity in all of our money affairs, and we have respect for our lives. Living debt-free makes everything better: our relationships, our family lives, our work, our ethics, and our values. All of it comes into alignment when we live debt-free.

This Book Is for You

This book was written for all debtors who, like me, couldn't see a way out. I offer you this book trusting that the Debt-Free Spending Plan will help you to achieve a life filled with freedom, peace, and self-directed happiness. You deserve it. The tools are here for the taking. Don't wait. Peace lies just around the bend.

when you're behind in, 59–61
see also Debt-Repayment Plan
peace, 241
  as benefit of debt-free living, 4,
    19, 20, 171
  with couples Spending Plan,
    145, 149, 154, 155, 158–160
  from funding things we love,
    82
  and integrity, 250
  lack of, 16
  in living with our money, 8
  from telling yourself the truth
    about money, 113
  with your payback timeline,
    135
personal coaching, 239
personal history
  debting and, 11
  and need for clarity, 18–19
personal loans, *see* family and
  personal loans
phone plans, 116
phones, cutting your spending on,
  115–116
planning, 15, 128, *see also* Debt-
  Free Spending Plan; Debt-
  Repayment Plan
prepared food, cutting your spending on, 98–99
presents, *see* gifts
pre-spending, 57, 60
pressure to overspend, for special
  events, 82–84, 87
produce, organic, 96–97
proportional spending, 91–92
  on Daily Needs, 44

in debt repayment, 125
living within your means as, 89
in wedding planning, 84
psychological spending issues, 10–11

realistic needs, 153
"rebuilding" credit, 247
receipts
  filing, 53
  organizing, 51
recessions
  and Healthy Reserve account,
    62–63
  and money issues, 19–20
record keeping
  for bankruptcy, 245
  tools for, 230–232
relationships
  being our true selves in, 149
  fear of uncertainty in, 139
  intimacy in, 154–156
  trouble with money in, 137–138,
    see also couple Debt-Free
    Spending Plan
rent, 121
repaying debt, *see* debt repayment
reserves
  for consultants, home office
    professionals, entrepreneurs,
    and artists, 63–65
  in Debt-Free Spending Plan, 4
  in Healthy Reserve account,
    62–65, 76–77
respect
  of family and friends who have
    loaned money, 165
  in partnerships, 154